WINTHROP FOUNDATIONS OF PUBLIC MANAGEMENT SERIES

Public Organization Behavior and Development

William B. Eddy
University of Missouri-Kansas City

Winthrop Publishers, Inc.
Cambridge, Massachusetts

Library of Congress Cataloging in Publication Data
Eddy, William B., 1933-
  Public organization behavior and development.

  (Foundations of public management series)
  Includes index.
  1. Public administration. 2. Organizational
change. 3. Organizational effectiveness. I. Title.
II. Series.
JF1411.E3   350.007   81-1136
ISBN 0-87626-741-X (cased ed.)   AACR2
ISBN 0-87626-740-1 (pbk.)

Design by David Ford

Winthrop Foundations of Public Management Series

© 1981 by Winthrop Publishers, Inc.
  17 Dunster Street, Cambridge, Massachusetts 02138

All rights reserved. No part of this book may be
reproduced in any form or by any means without
permission in writing from the publisher.

Printed in the United States of America

10 9 8 7 6 5 4 3 2 1

PUBLIC
ORGANIZATION
BEHAVIOR AND
DEVELOPMENT

For Bruce, Jill, and Martha

Contents

Foreword by Charles H. Levine   ix
Preface   xi

1. People in Public Organizations: Issues, Problems, Needs   1

Introduction/ Demands of Public Management/ Human Problems in Managing and Changing Contemporary Public Organizations/ Are Public Organizations Unique?/ Social Forces Affecting Public Agencies/ Learning about Organizations and Management/ Conclusion/ Notes to Chapter 1

2. History and Current Trends   17

Some Ancient History/ Bureaucracy and Structural Functionalism/ Scientific Management/ Civil Service and the Merit System/ The Human Relations Movement/ Applied Behavioral Science/ Conclusion/ Notes to Chapter 2

3. The Social Psychology of Work Behavior   40

Managing Behavior in Organizations/ Human Emotion and Motivation/ Other Emotional-Motivational Factors/ Attitudes and Values/ Stress/ Emotional Styles/ Perception/ Emotional Perception/ Self-Perceptions and

viii   Contents

Perceptions of Us by Others/ Other Problems in Perception/ Learning, Development, and Problem-Solving/ Learning: Intentional and Accidental/ Adult Learning and Career Development/ Conclusion/ Notes to Chapter 3

4. Structure and Process in Groups and Organizations   72

Structure/ Sociotechnical Systems/ A Model of Organization/ Human Interaction Processes/ Climate/ Influences on Process/ Groups in Organizations/ Human Needs and Organizational Demands/ Public and Private Systems/ Conclusion/ Notes to Chapter 4

5. Human Organizational Effectiveness   104

What Is Effectiveness?/ Individual Effectiveness/ Managerial Effectiveness/ The Effective Organization/ Conclusion/ Notes to Chapter 5

6. Leadership and Management   139

Situational Factors/ Power Distribution/ Managerial Styles/ Situational Contingencies in Managerial Performance/ Managerial Skills/ Motives of Successful Managers/ Management Development/ Ethical Issues in Public Management/ The Challenge of Public Management/ Notes to Chapter 6

7. Organization Development and Change   174

The Concept of Planned Change/ Alternatives for Planned Change/ Strategies for Planned Change/ Organization Development/ Organizational Change through Job Redesign/ Management by Objectives/ Imposed Change/ The Manager as a Change Agent/ Conclusion/ Notes to Chapter 7

Index   200

Foreword to the Winthrop Foundations of Public Management Series

Over the past several years growing interest and concern about the management of government have paralleled the growth of government itself. As a result, the study of public administration has been infused with new ideas and new approaches, giving it a new intellectual vitality and excitement. This has spread to those who must grapple with public problems as well as to those who study, teach, and conduct research about the public sector.

The books in the Winthrop Foundations of Public Management Series are intended to convey the new dynamism of public management. Each is intended to analyze a major aspect of public management—for example, intergovernmental relations, budgeting, human resources, decision making, organization behavior, and program management—by closely examining the blend of administrative, legal, political, and economic factors involved in producing government structures, processes, and outputs. The authors have approached their task by integrating the latest theoretical thinking with their empirical research to account for the behavior of public managers and organizations and the role of goals, functions, and norms in ongoing organizational arrangements. In every case the authors have stepped beyond the boundaries of a single discipline to search widely for perspectives, approaches, and research that might improve our understanding of public sector operations and enhance governmental performance.

The readers of this series—be they students taking an undergraduate course in public administration, those enrolled in a professional master's degree program, or people employed full time as public managers—should find the books uniformly readable, insightful, and useful. Readers should come to better understand and more fully appreciate the distinctive features of public management and organizations, and the difficulties involved in improving governmental performance in a democratic system that values accountability, equity, and rationality.

Charles H. Levine

Preface

Two decades ago I began my professorial career by straddling the academic fields of organizational psychology and public administration. I have never taken any formal courses in public administration but I have managed to survive, partly because my earliest mentor, Stanley Gabis, taught me how to communicate with public administrators. Partly because, also, many in the field are themselves spinoffs from political science and therefore tolerant of other hybrids—even one who had never read Max Weber or Chester Barnard.

One early choice I made has turned out to be a wise one—though it was accidental. It was the decision not to attempt to become a sort of public affairs Renaissance Man, encompassing the fields of public administration, political science, macroeconomics and behavioral science, but rather to remain a psychologist interested in applying my trade to people who work in public organizations.

This book follows that course. One of its aims is to help students who have limited formal background in the social and management sciences gain a foundation of knowledge about human behavior in organizational settings. A second aim is to provide the knowledge within a framework of public organizations. Thus the book is not about public organizations, but about the people who work in them. I do, of course, talk about public organizations as a necessary framework for understanding behavior, but the emphasis is not on painting a complete picture of the functioning of a public organization. Other books in the series will focus more directly on that topic.

The third aim of this book is to undertake the study from the *manager's* perspective—that is, from the point of view of the individual charged with taking action. There is an emphasis throughout on *doing* rather than on simply *describing*. And although I have tried to avoid being overly prescriptive, I have often discussed strategies for dealing with a problem area—though admittedly at a very general level.

My fourth aim relates to the last word of the title: development. We are at a point in the evolution of public management where the possibilities for organizational improvement go beyond the day-to-day decisions and reactions of the manager. They include longer-term programs and processes such as organization development, quality of work life, and management by objectives. I believe that it is important not only for students and managers to know about these technologies, but also for them to understand a little about how they relate to basic concerns in social science.

A final aim, important though usually addressed less directly, is to provide the reader with an opportunity to gain insight into his or her own managerial behavior. I hope that the questions asked and the issues posed will sometimes stimulate the reader to lay the book aside for a moment or two to muse about his or her own psychological needs, or leadership style, or ethical priorities.

I am thankful for the help of many people in bringing this work to completion. Charles Levine first proposed the basic idea, helped me focus my thinking, and provided valuable feedback on the first draft of the book. My colleague Dick Hermovics, who also works in both psychology and public administration, shared with me a number of thoughtful ideas about topics which need covering. Neely Gardner read the manuscript and provided many valuable substantive suggestions, as well as some much-appreciated support. An anonymous reviewer's feedback was sharp, but helpful in preventing several lacunae in the argument of the book. Dorothy Atkisson was heroic in typing the first draft, with assistance from Sibyl Storm, Joy Phillippe and Sherry Sullivan: and Norma Damon put it all into presentable shape. The copyeditor,

Martha Gleason, deserves your gratitude as well as mine for helping make the final product more readable.

Finally, special thanks go to my students, trainees and clients from public agencies who, over the years, have taught me what the real world of the public manager is like and have challenged me to continue striving to translate technical concepts and findings into usable and useful information.

1

People
in Public
Organizations:
Issues,
Problems,
Needs

INTRODUCTION

This book is about people who work in public organizations. Its aim is to help the reader learn more about why public employees behave the way they do, wht their concerns are, and what organizational factors affect them. We will discuss management skills, leadership strategies, and change techniques for administering more effectively. In addition, we will look at some of the issues that face public agencies in their efforts to utilize their human resources more effectively.

DEMANDS OF PUBLIC MANAGEMENT

The many organizational problems and pressures, plus the continuous search by managers and management scientists for improved methods, have led to an increasingly complex managerial role. Managers are asked to manage by objectives, to conduct performance-based appraisals, to perform team building with their work units, to function within a matrix structure, to utilize active listening while communicating, to encourage participative group decision making, and to be concerned about the social and environmental impacts of their actions. All this without any decrease in time or energy spent doing the job. It is not surprising that seminars about time management and coping with stress are popular!

For many managers, these concepts and tools did not exist when they went through their educational or training program in preparation for a managerial position. For others, the new strategies are only buzz words thrown around at seminars. Numerous public managers have told me, "These new techniques are like all the rest that come along every few months. They're OK if you have time for them, but I'm too busy putting out brush fires on a minute-to-minute basis."

A common dilemma is experienced by the manager who has received training in a technical or professional field such as engineering or nursing and finds that career progress is dependent upon managerial skills. The further one progresses in an organization, the greater the proportion of administrative/managerial chores that must be performed and the smaller the proportion of one's time is spent on the technical side. In fact, one significant cause of difficulty among young managers is the inability to give up the technical functions. Thus, the public manager who wishes to continue to progress must reconcile himself or herself to spending time and energy learning, and a significant aspect of that learning must involve human behavior in organizations.

The basic philosophy of this book is that not only are people the most important component of public organizations, but that people *are* public organizations. No matter what the objectives of an agency, human beings supply the driving force. All the other components (technology, structure, policies and procedures, physical resources, and so on) are there to assist the people in doing their jobs. There is ample evidence that the major attribute of successful managers is their ability to deal with subordinates in such a way that both productivity and satisfaction are enhanced. There is also ample evidence that when organizations begin to fail, it is frequently the case that something has gone wrong with the human part of the system—conflict, low commitment, poor coordination, or a plethora of other social interaction ills plague the organization and hamper its ability to utilize its other resources.

Later in this chapter I will discuss some of the differences between public and private organizations as they pertain to utilization of people and formulation of management techniques. First, however, we will propose the definition of a public organization to be utilized in this book. By public organization we will be referring to governmental agencies at all levels from local to federal (and in some cases international) and quasigovernmental agencies and government-sponsored institutions (such as veterans' hospitals), which are subject to the same kind of legislative oversight and civil service controls. We will also be referring to independent community service agencies run by boards of directors (often referred to as "third sector") and to voluntary associations or health care institutions, run by the government. It is my view that management strategies apply equally well to all these systems, but the contexts and conditioning factors may be different enough to require different operational techniques. Thus, the question of whether public and private organizations are significantly different from each other depends upon how general versus how specific you wish to be and also upon what aspects of the organization you focus on. Findings about human needs in organizational settings apply equally well to all, or at least most, organizations. Conversely, the study of budgeting techniques in a federal agency and in a small manufacturing firm would probably unearth some noticeable differences. Students whose primary interests are in nongovernmental agencies can feel comfortable starting their study with this volume, but should plan to augment it with additional readings.[1]

HUMAN PROBLEMS IN MANAGING AND CHANGING CONTEMPORARY PUBLIC ORGANIZATIONS

The last fifty years have been a period of high expectations and disappointments for governments in the Americas and many other countries. Ideals of egalitarianism, relatively plentiful resources, ambitious politicians, and well-organized constituencies and pressure groups have combined to formulate a major role for governments at all levels in improving the quality of life of the citizens. Government administrators have willingly tackled a variety of tasks, ranging from such limited and concrete duties as filling potholes in the streets and regulating meat packing to such expansive goals as overcoming the learning deficits of inner-city primary students and fine tuning the economy by adjusting the flow of capital. Not surprisingly, perhaps, all the goals have not been

4 Public Organization Behavior and Development

reached. Governments have come in for a good deal of criticism. A wide array of faults have been found with public organizations—often as much a function of the social or political views of the critic as the characteristics of the agency. Some criticisms have dealt with matters outside the scope of this book—political unresponsiveness, graft, and sheer size, to name a few. Some criticisms have focused on the human system, and we will review a few of these in order to better appreciate the problems of the public manager as he or she seeks to understand and utilize the employees of the agency.

Some of the human problems of contemporary public organizations with which the public managers must grapple include the following:

1. Inflexibility and inability to adapt to change. The basic assumptions of bureaucracy are based on the need for reliability and dependability. But these strengths can become weaknesses when the organization ia unable to change its ways of operating to meet new demands.[2]
2. Emphasis on control, rules, and compliance as opposed to problem solving and innovation. In order to assure efficient, accountable, and equitable performance, government organizations often proliferate large and complex systems of rules and procedures. Such organizations may then become rule-bound—more concerned with being self-protective and safe than with creating effective solutions to problems that arise.[3]
3. Employee overconcern with security. Civil service systems designed to protect employees from arbitrary meddling or dismissal by political groups have fostered a climate of safety consciousness and have also probably helped attract employees with high levels of concern for the basic needs for security and safety. Such a situation does not encourage an emphasis on achievement and innovation.
4. Inadequate renewal of human resources. Specialization and role orientation in public organizations often means that employees are fit into a slot where they stay unchallenged and unchanging until the natural processes of attrition promote them or retire them. There is not enough attention paid to the

need for providing developmental experiences such as training, job rotation, educational leaves, job enrichment, and career planning.
5. Hostile external constituents (politicians, citizen pressure groups, the media). It is common to criticize public employees without recognizing the devotion of most of them—thus generating a climate of low trust and confidence. Such views can permeate the agency, calling forth self-doubts, low morale, and the tendency to become self-protective.
6. Poor communication between top-level decision makers and first-line employees. There is often a large gap of understanding between those who make policies and those who are supposed to carry them out. Management systems that are highly centralized and nonparticipatory may not be able to inspire the workers to pursue the mission of the organization.
7. Poor collaboration among groups within the agency and with other agencies. Because of specialization, low mobility, jealousy about territory, and other factors, groups may become insulated from others and expend more energy guarding their boundaries or competing than building cooperative arrangements with other units. This causes the organization and its subunits to be closed to needs for joint action.
8. Reactive problem avoiding rather than proactive problem finding. Some agencies deploy their human resources mainly toward responding to pressures and crises that arise rather than planning and building ways of identifying problems and heading them off before they become critical.
9. Employees whose primary loyalties are to other organizations. Many public agencies have merit systems that are designed to assure that employees are hired on the basis of qualifications rather than political affiliations or interest group membership. Some, however, do not. Managers in these organizations have their jobs considerably complicated by their inability to exert control over subordinates. Some public employee associations or unions similarly compete for employees' loyalty.[4]
10. Lack of leadership-managerial resources. Individuals who are specialists or professionals are often promoted into supervisory positions because of accumulated tenure or as a reward

for technical performance. In too many organizations these people are managers only by label—they do not have the knowledge or skills necessary to lead others effectively.

These conditions cause problems between the public organization and its constituencies (such as citizens or clients). Services are not delivered, problems are not solved, responses are delayed, and regulations are not enforced equitably. The dilemmas also bring about internal stresses. Conflicts arise and go unresolved, people are "turned off" and retreat into their shells, concern develops for appearances or images rather than for success itself, creative people leave if they can.

ARE PUBLIC ORGANIZATIONS UNIQUE?

There is an old maxim in the management consulting field to the effect that while all organizations believe themselves to be unique and different, they are, in fact, basically similar. Scholars have tended to be more convinced that there are significant differences —especially scholars in public administration who have felt it important to differentiate the field of public management from the better developed field of business administration. Public managers themselves also tend to perceive differences between public and private organizations. They cite such realities as the fact that public agencies usually do not produce a physical product and do not pursue a profit and thus find it difficult to evaluate their performance objectively. Or that policies and agency goals are often set by outside legislative bodies rather than an internal board of directors and are thus further out of the control of the manager.

The question of whether public and private organizations are different is really a moot point—they are different in some ways and similar in others. And, of course, there are many differences among various kinds of public and third sector agencies. For the purpose of this book, however, there is a slightly different question: What implications, if any, do the unique aspects of public agencies have for the human dimensions such as supervisory techniques, employee attitudes, and programs for change and development?

Managers and employees of public organizations increasingly find that they function in *open* sociotechnical systems. Forces outside the agency as well as the usual internal factors must be reckoned with. At all levels of government there is conflict between administrators, whose purposes are better suited by maintaining a traditional, efficient, closed system approach, and external agents (interest groups, media, consumer advocates, politicians), who believe that efficient operation is second to mission accomplishment or responsiveness to various needs and who wish to see the system as being open to outside influence. The following list, while not totally exhaustive, serves the purpose of highlighting most of the differences that will be pertinent to our discussion. It has been compiled from the work of several authorities. You will note that some of the factors have been referred to earlier in a different context.

1. Performance criteria. Private businesses (except for monopolies and oligopolies) are rewarded on the basis of how well they satisfy customer needs or wants. In contrast, agencies are supported out of governmental budget allocations, which are usually much less directly tied to performance and more related to efficiency, demonstrated effort, promises, and so on. Such a process makes it more difficult to evaluate performance and to reward on that basis.
2. Accessibility to external influence. Public agencies are vulnerable to inputs and pressures from many constituents and pressure groups that may find their way into the organization through a variety of different portals. Since public agencies are open systems, what goes on inside (policies, budget allocations, personnel decisions) may be legitimately influenced by outsiders. While things are changing somewhat, business organizations are typically more closed, with few controlled points or access—such as the board of directors, marketing department, and various operations affected by government regulations. Public employees may find themselves subject to conflicting priorities and values.
3. Greater internal diversity. Ideally, organizations are constructed so that all the subunits mesh together into a well-coordinated whole. For many public agencies this ideal does not hold.

Because of political factors, historical coincidences, or new demands, many agencies are composed of diverse specialized groups that are only vaguely and indirectly related to the same set of goals. Sometimes even the goals are in conflict—as, for example, the U.S. government's price support program for tobacco versus its efforts to discourage smoking.

4. Conflict between policymakers and administrators. In the public sector most broad policy is made, or at least ratified, by elected officials—politicians. In theory, at least, the policy is then carried out by administrators and their subordinates. Although there is not the clear-cut distinction between the policy process and the administrative process that high school civics books once implied, there is often a division between the people who see their roles as policymaking and those whose job is management. Since the two groups have different missions, respond to different pressures, and are rewarded for different functions, it is to be expected that there is likely to be mistrust and conflict. While no claim is made that the relationship between a corporate board of directors and the top executives of a firm is totally harmonious with no overlap, the administrative-political mix in public agencies seems to be a more difficult problem.

5. The employment contract. In most governmental agencies and some third sector groups, employees operate in a special relationship to the organization. In times past and in some present-day organizations, *patronage* (the *spoils system*) dictates that employees are hired, protected, and promoted on the basis of their political activities. In many modern public organizations, however, the civil service system operates. Employees are hired on the basis of technical qualifications, but the process often becomes a highly protective one in which seniority figures heavily in promotions, and firing can take place only after exhaustive documentation and hearings. In the private sector unions sometimes fulfill some of the same functions as do civil service regulations, but the firm can usually act somewhat more independently and arbitrarily when evaluating and dealing with employees.

6. Scrutiny by media and public interest groups. The fact that public agencies utilize tax funds to implement public policies

People in Public Organizations: Issues, Problems, Needs

in a democratic society makes them targets for investigation by outside groups. The continuous risk of exposure of internal matters makes them prone to spend energy covering up and seeking to protect themselves. Consequences include lowered willingness to risk new techniques and avoidance of dealing with conflicts and other interpersonal issues. Business organizations are much less subject to such scrutiny of their internal processes (although, of course, their policies and procedures in areas such as personnel selection, safety, fair employment, and environmental impact are increasingly examined).

7. Emphasis on stability and reliability. The strong emphasis in public agencies is most often on accountability, efficiency, and legality, rather than upon maximum effectiveness or flexibility. Although agencies are subject to more drastic changes in leadership because of elections than are businesses, their internal mechanisms are commonly perceived to be more resistant to change.

8. Emphasis on fast and visible demonstrations of progress. The time horizon in public organizations tends to be from one election to another—usually two to four years. Budgets are drawn up annually. Thus there is pressure on managers to demonstrate results quickly for purposes of political support. This often sacrifices long-range planning and investment in development programs for crisis responses and programs that are less solid but more appealing. Businesses are not free from this tendency, but the external pressures usually are not as great and longer range planning is more likely.

9. Emphasis on strong individual leadership. Folk wisdom, often reinforced by the media, places very strong emphasis on the need for strong, charismatic, assertive leadership of public institutions. There are very significant external pressures on elected and appointed leaders to demonstrate their personal power. Delegation of responsibility, heavy reliance on staff, and group decision making are often viewed as weaknesses. Although conventional business executives would not be very different, they are less visible and are subject to less pressure to appear authoritative and personally responsible.

10. Atmosphere of control and mistrust. Since agencies must

emphasize accountability and honesty, there are often many rules and regulations that place strict controls on employees. These rules are usually written for the lowest common denominator, that is, the employee who is least capable and/or least trustworthy. Also, there may be various internal policing systems for checking on compliance—with the apparent assumption that the employees will misbehave if they think they can get away with it. Businesses are certainly not free from this condition—some are no doubt as mistrustful as agencies—but wherever the condition occurs, it may become characteristic of the overall organizational climate. Thus, the capable and trustworthy employees are painted with the same brush as the cheaters and, some observers suggest, may ultimately begin to act the way they think the agency expects them to act—unmotivated and uncaring.

11. Government employment as welfare. There exists in some people's minds, and in some agencies, the philosophy that one purpose of government is to provide employment to citizens who are otherwise unemployable because of marginal qualifications, handicaps, or membership in a minority group. This belief cannot help but affect the nature of the work force. Currently, laws and regulations also exert pressure on business to hire disadvantaged persons, but there is more provision for their hiring the best qualified, rather than the least qualified, from marginal groups.

12. Differences in status. Although changes are taking place in some areas, it has generally been felt that working for the government is a lower status occupation than working for business or industry, or in a profession. While salaries in the federal government are quite competitive with the private sector for most levels, scales in many local, state, and human service organizations are lower. In addition, there is a tendency for public employees to be viewed as being interested primarily in easy and secure jobs ("feeding at the public trough"). This attitude may provide an obstacle to the manager who is attempting to build up the morale and commitment of the work unit.

It should be noted before leaving this topic that there are many similarities between public and private organizations. It is common for a business leader to accept an assignment in government and subsequently to proclaim in surprise that government employees are fully as qualified, devoted, and energetic as were those in the private sector work force. The basic principles of human psychology, as well as those of accounting, personnel administration, and leadership, apply to both. As a matter of fact, two recent studies found high degrees of similarity between the roles of public and private managers. Those in both groups function similarly in regard to functions performed, complexity, and pressures.[5] There are times when the similarities can even cause difficulty. The tendency on the part of a business manager to want to promote his or her department to grow—with a bigger budget, more employees, more physical space, and so on, is viewed as a good old American ambition. For a public manager to act on these same societal values in these days of concern about governmental expenditures is liable to be viewed as wasteful and adventuresome.[6]

It should be pointed out that some observers assert that distinctions between public and private organizations are decreasing over time. Industries are being pressured to function in many ways beyond merely manufacturing and selling products. They must cope with environmental concerns, community betterment, international relations, and fair employment. Meanwhile, governmental agencies find themselves operating high technology ventures such as transportation systems and research and development laboratories. Further, there are an increasing number of "quasi-governmental" organizations which do not clearly fit into the traditional categories of either government or business. These include Amtrak, the Telstar satellite communication system, the Postal Service, and the Tennessee Valley Authority. Thus, the more useful focus of study would seem to be to seek to understand the *general* principles of behavior which underlie most, if not all, organizations and then to learn to discern the significant unique characteristics of any organization under study, whether it be public or private.

SOCIAL FORCES AFFECTING PUBLIC AGENCIES

In addition to the problems discussed above, having to do with attitudes and reactions of employees, the public manager is also faced with a variety of social and legislative issues relating to the employees. Public employee unions are growing in size, strength, and militancy. They have insisted on participating not only in discussions of economic rewards, but also in matters of employee rights, limitations on the authority of supervisors, working conditions, and work design. Public managers of all levels have had to learn not only how to deal with individual employees but also with their bargaining units. Many of the traditional leverage points for dealing with employees are taken away from the supervisor in collective bargaining situations and are vested in staff experts in personnel and industrial relations functions.

Another social issue that is beginning to impinge on the manager is concern for *quality of work life.* A landmark study by the U.S. Department of Health, Education, and Welfare in 1972[7] showed that a significant proportion of American workers—both managers and nonsupervisory employees—were dissatisfied with their jobs and with their careers. Other studies and industrial experiences supported the finding that many employees believe their jobs to be more dull, confining, unrewarding, and stressful than they should be. Findings in Europe by the Quality of Work Life Foundation have supported these attitudes. There is emerging the concept of *organizational citizenship.* Workers are increasingly being seen as citizens of the organization with certain rights and privileges, not just temporary hired hands. The expectations of employees may include such concerns as employment security, participation in decision making (sometimes including policymaking), measures to make work more interesting and less stressful, and financial support for training necessary for advancement. As these influences permeate organizations, the manager will be called upon to function in ways dramatically different from the methods of traditional administrators who held most of the power. For example, in some European countries, laws have recently been passed that require a certain percentage of corporate boards of directors to be comprised of employees.

A third influence is the increasing emphasis on legislation and policies to protect and enhance the opportunities of subgroups, minorities, women, older workers, the handicapped, veterans, and youth. Hardly a week goes by without reports of a court case that affirms the rights of a subgroup member to special treatment to overcome a disadvantage. Discriminatory employment tests are prohibited, as are selection standards that cannot be proved to link directly to job performance. For example, recent court decisions have held that under many circumstances race, sex, citizenship, age, religion, and marital status may not be considered in hiring decisions. In the landmark *Griggs* v. *Duke Power Company* case the U.S. Supreme Court ruled that a selection test that is biased by race, color, or other cultural factors (as most are) cannot be used unless validity studies clearly indicate the importance of the abilities measured for a particular job.[8] Special training or retraining can be required to help overcome inadequate educational backgrounds. Quotas for the hiring and promotion of minority group members are frequently imposed, and the onus is on the manager to defend any deviation.

Yet another social phenomenon that impinges upon the manager is the changing attitude about work. Earlier in this century, when the industrial revolution was at its apex, societal values supported the kind of behavior required to "fit in" to the work place. Horatio Alger gained fame by writing tales of young men who rose from rags to riches through hard work and obedience. In his book *Future Shock* Alvin Toffler asserts that even the public schools are geared to conditioning people to work well in factories (being on time, working hard without talking, obeying orders, and so on).[9] These attitudes are changing—especially among younger workers. For a variety of reasons there is less willingness to obey authority simply because "it's the right thing to do." People want to be told why and also to be asked their opinions. There is less tolerance for arbitrary measures based on management's prerogatives and more demands for participation in decision making. Workers feel much more justified in asserting their individual needs and their rights to some say-so about measures that affect them. Under the theme "industrial humanism" some critics are even challenging the rights of management to serve the demands of the organization as opposed to the needs of the individuals.

There are still other trends that affect the ways workers relate to their jobs. These include today's welfare and unemployment compensation systems, which take a large measure of the dire threat away from losing one's job; the high incidence of working couples—each of whom can provide a sustaining income if the other leaves the job; and the greater demands for work efficiency triggered by rising costs and taxpayers' resistance to increased funding. Rather than continue to describe changes, however, it seems important to explore the significance of the above changes on the manager. There was a time when the manager could wield a good deal of direct power. He or she could determine who was hired and fired. how much raise was given, the way the job was to be done, and he could mete out punishment in a variety of forms. Now many of these functions are controlled by laws, regulations, and other persons. The manager is left with very little direct power. The personnel department does the hiring, utilizing job specifications established by a consulting firm and qualification standards set by the law. The manager may be allowed to interview the candidates and may or may not make the final selection. Performance standards are established by outside experts, sometimes in collaboration with the managers; wage rates and raises are determined by collective bargaining; employee rights are protected by a legion of boards, panels, and regulations; and firing requires a long series of steps—possibly including court action.

These limitations on the ability of the manager to influence employees through regulations and rewards and punishments place a premium on *leadership skills*. The creation of a stable, productive, and satisfied work force is increasingly dependent on such factors as understanding human behavior, good communication skills, effectiveness in meetings and other group settings, ability to conduct productive appraisal and goal-setting interviews, and techniques for dealing with conflict. In short, managers and supervisors in the kinds of public organizations we have been describing must rely largely on their own behavior and on the work climate they establish to influence their subordinates.

LEARNING ABOUT ORGANIZATIONS AND MANAGEMENT

This book is intended as an aid to learning about human behavior in organizations. A note of caution is necessary, however. In fact— two notes. In the first place, there is a big difference between studying *about* an activity and actually performing that activity. Numerous studies have demonstrated that theoretical learning in the classroom does not necessarily carry over to work. There are several reasons for this unhappy truth, including the facts that (1) skill and knowledge are not the same things, (2) real situations are more complex (contain more variables) than textbook examples, and (3) students may encounter resistances to implementing their learning that they do not have the power to overcome. This is why management educational and training programs are increasingly utilizing experience-based learning activities—exercises, simulations, skill practice, applied research projects, and so on. It also accounts in part for the growing popularity of organization development (OD), an approach that utilizes actual work units or teams within the organization as the learning groups—thus assuring that the learnings are discussed and practiced in the setting in which they are to be utilized.

The second note of caution pertains to the fit between the theory and the learner's own personality and style of interacting. It is wise to go slowly and carefully in attempting to apply new techniques. The statement that "a majority of successful managers utilize teamwork" should not, for example, be taken as a mandate for the reader to call everyone together for a meeting. It could better be taken as a worthwhile avenue to explore in regard to the manager's own skill with groups as well as its applicability to a given situation.

CONCLUSION

In this chapter we have discussed some of the considerations involved in the study of people in organizations. It is evident that organizations are complex entities—sociotechnical systems of interacting people and technology. Maximizing productivity and work satisfaction requires more than setting up procedures and initiating new programs. Managing involves an understanding of the behavior of people as well as the skill to put the knowledge into practice.

NOTES TO CHAPTER 1

1. See Richard Steiner, *Managing the Human Service Organization*, Beverly Hills, Calif.: Sage, 1977. Also see Peter F. Drucker, *An Introductory View of Management*, (Part 2, Performance in the Service Institution, pp. 128-165), New York: Harper, 1977.

2. This point of view has been forcefully presented by Warren Bennis in *Changing Organizations*, New York: McGraw-Hill, 1966.

3. Robert Merton's conception of the *bureaupathic personality* was that some organizations become so rule-bound and oriented toward safety that the environment actually affects the personalities of the employees. See his *Social Theory and Social Structure*, Glencoe, Ill.: The Free Press, 1949.

4. David T. Stanley, "The Ambiguous Role of the Urban Public Employee," in Charles H. Levine (ed.), *Urban Affairs Annual Review. Managing Human Resources*, vol. 13, Beverly Hills, Calif.: Sage, 1977.

5. James W. Driscoll, G. L. Cowger, and R. J. Egan, "Private Managers and Public Myths—Public Managers and Private Myths," *Sloan Management Review*, Fall 1969, pp. 53–57. Also see Alan W. Lau, A. R. Newman, and L. A. Broedling, "The Nature of Managerial Work in the Public Sector," *Public Administration Review*, vol. 40, 1980, pp. 513–520.

6. Discussions of differences between public and private organizations are common in the literature. For other views related to human resources see R. T. Golembiewski, "Organization Development in Public Agencies: Perspectives on Theory and Practice," *Public Administration Review*, vol. 29, July–August 1969, pp. 367–377, and E. J. Giblin, "Organization Development: Public Sector Theory and Practice," *Public Personnel Management*, vol. 5, no. 2, March–April 1976, pp. 112–119.

7. U.S. Department of Health, Education, and Welfare, *Work in America*, Report to the Secretary of a Special Task Force, Washington, D.C., 1972.

8. See David H. Rosenbloom, "The Public Employee in Court: Implications for Urban Government," in C. H. Levine (ed.), *Urban Affairs Annual Review. Managing Human Resources*, vol. 13, Beverly Hills, Calif.: Sage, 1977.

9. Alvin Toffler, *Future Shock*, New York: Random House, 1970.

2
History and Current Trends

If, as we have asserted, people are the critical element in public organizations, it seems useful to gain a clear picture of what makes public employees behave the way they do. Behavior can best be understood by looking at the human being in the context of his or her sociotechnical environment. This chapter aims to set the stage for such understanding by providing a background and a present-day framework. Through such a treatment of the environment of the public employee, the reader will, I hope, be able to appreciate both the uniqueness of the public sector work place and the communalities the public employee shares with other workers everywhere.

SOME ANCIENT HISTORY

If one traces history back far enough, distinctions between public and private employment blur, as do differences between work and play as well as work and religious practice. In the most ancient civilizations, people were hunters and foodgatherers. They roamed in bands or tribes, probably spending most of their waking hours doing what was necessary to survive. Later with the advent of agriculture they tended to stay in one place longer and to build larger and more complex communities.[1] In both kinds of systems, however, people no doubt discovered the need to *organize*—to find ways to *direct* and *coordinate* their collective efforts toward a *group goal* such as harvesting food. As Presthus observes in his discussion of modern bureaucracies, "All organizations are made up of two basic elements—people and their functional roles."[2] This fact was no less true 10,000 years ago. As long as members of the community had different duties and responsibilities (or roles), such as tending the crops, caring for children, chasing away wild animals, or ministering to the sick, there were the early vestiges of organizations, and thus there were *management problems*.

We have no reason to believe that members of ancient civilizations were basically different from human beings of today. Thus, they no doubt faced many of the same issues in attempting to coordinate human behavior in organizations. Members who played differing roles did not automatically mesh their efforts with others. Someone had to see that that happened or else those who were to separate the grain from the straw might not be on hand when it was brought in from the field. Or the children, if not kept quiet and confined at certain times, might scare the animals that were being hunted. Some power more encompassing than that of a single person or subunit had to oversee and coordinate the big picture.

Another problem, we speculate, was that all the various jobs or roles that needed doing were not seen as equally desirable. Some were more demanding or dangerous or boring. Again, there had to be some force which assured that the necessary roles were played. Things could not always be left to personal taste or whim when the welfare of the entire tribe was at stake.

Problems such as those we have described called for some form of *authority* supported by a system of *rules* and *procedures*. Since daily fights to see whose will is to prevail make life too unpredictable, some more permanent rationale for authority needed to be found. Various tribes and communities over time evolved different criteria for who should lead, but they usually had to do with some measure of *fitness*—age, wisdom, victories, physical feats, and so on. And, since the leader couldn't be in all places at once, he (or occasionally, she) passed *rules* to represent his authority in absentia. The rules could then be enforced by assistant leaders, often sons, who derived their power from the endorsement of the main leader. And, of course, there had to be rewards and punishments to assure that the rules were followed and the wishes of the leader carried out. Sometimes these were justified through religious systems.

It is no doubt apparent that even the earlier forms of organizations—tribes and communities—were confronted with many of the same management issues that confront us today and that many of the same strategies were used. We have noted coordination, role differentiation, compliance, authority, rules and rewards, and punishments. Others that we have not mentioned include planning (some historians believe agriculture provided humanity with its first major need for planning), systems of communication, specialization, selection, and record keeping.

As we mentioned earlier, in ancient civilizations there was not much distinction between what we think of today as the major institutions of society. Government and religion were either the same or highly intertwined. Except for feudal estates, few private organizations of any size existed until the industrial revolution of the 1700s, and military organizations often controlled all the others. There was relatively little writing about employee relations, but there was a good deal of concern about the rights and protection of citizens. One of the significant human dilemmas was then, as now, how to regulate authority. Without the coordinating and controlling influences of an authority system, tribes or communities became disorganized and survival was threatened. But once in place, authority systems tend to become self-perpetuating and power-oriented and to victimize the followers they were originally supposed to help.

From the times of the tribes and communities of antiquity through the early civilizations of Egypt, China, Greece, and Rome, forms of human organization became larger, more complex, and more imbued with technology. These cultures, which existed two to seven thousand years ago, further established and refined the knowledge of how to get things done through cooperative effort. The early civilizations consisted of builders, traders, and soldiers. They built huge structures without the aid of power machinery, they navigated the seven seas, and they ruled over far-flung kingdoms acquired by large armies. Such operations required sophisticated techniques for controlling and coordinating the behavior of their members.

The writings from these civilizations reveal the attempts of leaders in government and military organizations to understand and influence the behavior of the people. George chronicles several interesting examples. In a school book an ancient Egyptian advised on how to deal with complaints through what we today call *active listening*

> If thou art one to whom petition is made, be calm as thou listenest to what the petitioner has to say. Do not rebuff him before he has swept out his body or before he has said that for which he came. . . . It is not [necessary] that everything about which he has petitioned should come to pass, [but] a good hearing is soothing to the heart.[3]

San Tzu, Chinese military authority, wrote the following in 50 B.C. in regard to the need for clear communication:

> *On Directing* If the words of command are not clear and distinct, if orders are not thoroughly understood, the general is to blame. But if his orders are clear, and the soldiers nevertheless disobey, then it is the fault of their officers.[4]

And, finally, this excerpt from a dialogue between Socrates and Nicomachides on the topic of the duties of the manager in regard to how to handle the followers:

> "I say," said Socrates, "that over whatever a man may preside, he will if he knows what he needs, and is able to provide it, be a good president, whether he have the direction of a chorus, a family, a city, or an army."
>
> "By Jupiter, Socrates," cried Nicomachides, "I should never have expected to hear from you that good managers of a family would also be good generals."
>
> "Come, then," proceeded Socrates, "let us consider what are the duties of each of them, that we may understand whether they are the same, or are in any respect different."
>
> "By all means," he said.
>
> "Is it not, then, the duty of both," asked Socrates, "to render those under their command obedient and submissive to them?"
>
> "Unquestionably."
>
> "Is it not also the duty of both to appoint fitting persons to fulfill the various duties?"
>
> "That is also unquestionable."
>
> "To punish the bad, and to honour the good, too, belongs, I think to each of them."
>
> "Undoubtedly."
>
> "And is it not honourable in both to render those under them well-disposed towards them?"
>
> "That also is certain."

"And do you think it for the interest of both to gain for themselves allies and auxiliaries or not?"[5]

These writings, plus many other similar ones, indicate an interest not only in rules and structures, but also in behavior. How can one best deal with people in order to elicit cooperation, hard work, and devotion?

It is probably true, of course, that the general social conditions and value systems of the times supported a highly authoritarian, centralized, and hierarchical form of organization. Many people were untrained and uneducated and, indeed, were serfs or slaves. Class lines and caste systems in societies were duplicated in military and governmental organizations. And the use of raw power was seen as not only legitimate but also necessary in order to maintain order and assure that organizations stayed intact and the necessary work got done. The general assumption was that the power was rightfully vested in those at the top of the organization (the *divine right* of kings). If they were benevolent, they could choose to treat their subordinates well, in return for which they hoped to receive a higher level of *esprit de corps* and greater effort. They also needed to strive to understand the principles of motivation that govern the behavior of members so that they could use appropriate mixtures of reward and punishment to control their work behavior. There was usually both a fairly clear distinction between leaders and followers and an assumption that the followers were interested in working only to receive wages or to avoid some threat or penalty.

Niccolo Machiavelli characterized well the prevailing attitudes about employees. Writing in the sixteenth century—a time that marked the transition between the medieval period and the beginning of the modern era—he recorded the principles of leadership and power that had evolved in the city-states. His principle of *mass consent* stressed the importance of winning the approval of the followers and of deriving strength from the grassroots. However, his view (or, more precisely, his picture of the prevailing values of the times) was that in order to hold on to his power, the leader is justified in using whatever manipulating or controlling methods are necessary. The followers are to be listened to and mollified, but they are clearly still the followers and the leader's job is to control them.

BUREAUCRACY AND STRUCTURAL FUNCTIONALISM

As the industrial revolution progressed, city-states became countries, military organizations and churches grew in size and complexity, and a new organizational form evolved. No longer could a strong leader and a few loyal lieutenants or staff members control an entire organization by making all the decisions and keeping an eye on everyone. Things were too spread out. Too many areas required technical knowledge, and delays caused by waiting on direct orders to deal with every circumstance were too costly. And so, large organizations had to be divided up into subunits, each of which had a specialized function and each managed by individuals who had the knowledge to oversee that particular function.

Max Weber, the German social scientist, studied the large-scale organizations that existed in the latter part of the nineteenth century. He observed that one of their distinguishing characteristics was that they were built up out of *bureaus* (offices) and had to place major emphasis on a system of rules and controls for coordinating the widely divergent activities. Indeed, the term *bureaucracy* referred originally to such a collection of bureaus or specialized offices that characterized a large-scale organization. Our present-day use of the term to connote an overly cumbersome and rule-bound system has derived from some of the side effects of such an organization.

Weber further characterized the bureaucracy as having the following distinct features:

1. "The regular activities required for the purpose of the organization are distributed in a fixed way as official duties." Specialization of both units and individuals, based on the principle of division of labor, fixes responsibility for a segment of the work.
2. "The organization of offices follows the principle of hierarchy; that is each lower office is under the control and supervision of a higher one." Each member of the *chain of command* is responsible for and accountable for the work of his subordinates.
3. "Operations are governed by a consistent system of abstract rules and consist of the application of these rules to particular

cases." Reliability and uniformity are assured by rules that apply to *all* cases equally. Members are protected from arbitrary or capricious actions.
4. "The ideal official conducts his office in a state of *formalistic impersonality* . . . without hatred or passion, and hence without affection or enthusiasm." To allow feelings to find their way into administrative matters allows for subjectivity and impartiality and thus hampers efficiency.
5. "Employment in the bureaucratic organization is based on technical qualifications and is protected against arbitrary dismissal." These personnel policies promote loyalty and stability of the work force.[6]

Weber believed that the ideal bureaucratic organization he described was technically capable of achieving the highest level of efficiency. It would use the most qualified and specialized personnel, detach itself from emotionality, and do other things to achieve a high degree of rationality. Although such an approach may seem restrictive to us today, it was viewed in its time as an advance over arbitrary feudal practices.

Weber did not invent bureaucracy, he only studied and labeled it. Neither did he believe it constituted the perfect form of human organization. He worried about the impact of bureaucratic mechanisms on individual autonomy, and is quoted as lamenting:

It is horrible to think that the world could one day be filled with nothing but those little cogs, little men clinging to little jobs and striving towards bigger ones—a state of affairs which is to be seen once more, as in the Egyptian records, playing an ever-increasing part in the spirit of our present administrative system, and especially of its offspring, the students. This passion for bureaucracy . . . is enough to drive one to despair. It is as if in politics . . . we were deliberately to become men who need "order" and nothing but order, who become nervous and cowardly if for one moment this order wavers, and helpless if they are torn away from their total incorporation in it. That the world should know no men but these: it is in such an evolution that we are already caught up, and the great question is therefore not how we can promote and hasten it, but what can we oppose to this machinery in order to keep a portion of mankind free from this parcelling-out of the soul, from this supreme mastery of the bureaucratic way of life.[7]

A number of American and English experts on organization and management followed a point of view similar to Weber's, but pushed more in the direction of developing *prescriptive*, or "how to," recommendations for structuring organizations. These writings, sometimes called theories of *administrative management*, included such pioneers as Luther Gulick, Lyndall Urwick, and Charles Babbage. In later years Ernest Dale, writing for the American Management Association, has continued this tradition. This viewpoint placed the emphasis on designing the formal structure of the organization through the use of organization charts, systems and procedures manuals, and flow diagrams. They were also concerned with discovering universal rules of management that assured maximum efficiency. Such concepts as *unity of command* (one man-one boss), *span of control* (one person can supervise a maximum number of employees), and *chain of command* (the hierarchy of authority) are examples of these principles. In attempting to help the manager understand how to maintain control over the system, Gulick created the acronym **POSDCORB** which asserted that the functions of management are: Planning, Organization, Staffing, Directing, COordinating, Reporting, Budgeting.[8]

These notions about how best to organize contained an implicit set of assumptions about the people who were employees. The belief was that a well-designed, rational organization should function smoothly and efficiently, like a well-oiled machine. Workers tended to be thought of as rather depersonalized cogs—so much so that later critics have labeled these theories "theories of organizations without people." Insofar as possible the work to be done was divided into specialized subunits and employees were given narrowly defined duties. Modern managers specialized in developing complete job descriptions and control mechanisms to keep track of employees to be sure they did their jobs. The ethic of the times was that "work is the curse of the common man" and therefore no one really could be expected to enjoy a job. It was necessary to hold a job in order to live and support one's family, but there was usually little expectation of any other reward. Social scientists and writers became interested in the impact of work on laborers and worried about the effects of large organizations on human development.

In an era of consistent economic development wage rates rose steadily—if slowly. But the growing strength of unions in the

1920s and 1930s demonstrated that all was not well, and many managers wondered why workers weren't satisfied.

SCIENTIFIC MANAGEMENT

A development that paralleled and complemented administrative management was Frederick W. Taylor's *scientific management*.[9] Taylor, an engineer, sought to apply principles of scientific investigation from such fields as physics and physiology to the design of work. Although Taylorism is now often seen as an effort to turn workers into human robots, Taylor's motives were quite different. In his writings around the turn of the century he noted that workers' jobs were usually designed in very subjective fashion using rules of thumb rather than scientific procedures. His belief was that if jobs were properly studied and engineered, workers could do them more easily and quickly and thus earn more wages. He pioneered what has come to be called *time and motion study* and the piece rate system for rewarding people on the basis of their units of output.

Taylor's work and that of his followers Frank and Lillian Gilbreth had a major impact on American organizations and on the development of such modern techniques as operations research, management science, and decision sciences.[10] The quantitative approach to the design and measurement of work processes now taken for granted is one of the legacies of these pioneers. Another legacy is a view of human motivation that is somewhat simplistic and incomplete, but that was consistent with the general beliefs of the time. Taylor's assumption was that workers are motivated by economic desires and that a system of monetary rewards and punishments was what was needed to raise productivity as well as morale. In fairness to Taylor it should be noted that he also advocated scientifically devised selection and training programs, fair and consistent standards of performance, and greater cooperation between workers and management. It has also been pointed out that many workers in organizations of Taylor's time were illiterate immigrants who could not cope with advancing technologies unless jobs were engineered to be simple and routine.[11] Nevertheless, the view of the worker as an economically motivated dependent adjunct to the mechanical system prevailed for several decades—and in fact persists in some organizations today.

CIVIL SERVICE AND THE MERIT SYSTEM

People who worked in public agencies were significantly influenced by the ideas of Taylor and the administrative management theorists. But, in addition, a set of beliefs about government employment was developing and was also to have a major impact.

The management in a public agency is typically more unstable and transitory than in privately owned business because of the impact of periodic elections and also because of the scrutiny of the media for possible wrongdoing. This has historically created a desire on the part of politicians, managers, and workers to do what they can to ensure the continuation of their employment. One of the solutions to the uncertainty has been a symbiotic relationship between all parties, often referred to as patronage politics or the *spoils system*. Under such a system the primary criteria for selecting a worker is his or her affiliation with the party in power and demonstrated willingness to lend support in the form of money and service. Technical qualifications come second. Party workers are rewarded with jobs for their loyalty. In turn, they support the politicians politically as well as administratively, thereby preserving the political organization and thus everyone's job and power.[12]

There are a few advantages to the spoils system. It presumably stays in close touch with the grass roots and is more responsive to the problems and needs of the citizens. Also, it is reputed to be more capable of supporting the platform of the elected party than would be a group of neutral employees. And, finally, in the days before modern personnel systems, it served as a mechanism for recruiting and channeling manpower into government. However, there are distinct disadvantages that, for many, clearly outweigh the advantages.

Probably the most obvious problem with the spoils system is the practice of selecting workers and managers on the basis of political affiliations rather than ability to do the job. Such a practice can waste taxpayers' money by populating the agency with unqualified personnel, discourage competent professionals from seeking government employment, and divert the efforts of the agency away from its official mission into supporting the political careers of its officials. As technology has advanced and both the missions and operations of government have become more complex, the tolerance for semiqualified patronage employees has decreased. For example, while we might tend to shrug off the information that poorly qualified patronage employees infest the county parks department, most of us would not put up with such people designing our highway bridges, operating airport control towers, or auditing banks.

From the point of view of the employee there is another disadvantage of the spoils system. That is the fact that in spite of one's commitment to support the political leadership of the agency, employment is still somewhat unpredictable and subject to arbitrary actions of the leaders. Even though one works hard and performs the job well, there is no guarantee that political changes or the whim of an official will not cause the loss of a job or perhaps demotion to a less desirable position. Other accusations against the spoils system are that it encourages graft and can be more easily bought by special interest groups.

The answer to the spoils system was the emerging bureaucracy described by Weber. As agencies grew and assumed increasingly important and complex roles, the problems attendant to an unstable and semiqualified work force became unacceptable to most people. In the latter half of the nineteenth century in the United States the civil service reform movement became a strong force. Such events as President Garfield's assassination by an unsuccessful spoils office seeker helped to consolidate opinions. In 1883 the Pendleton Act established a Civil Service Commission to administer competitive examinations to job seekers in order to select the most qualified regardless of political affiliation. This step was instrumental in reinforcing the concept of employment based on merit, but it also was the beginning of a philosophy that an employee of government under a merit system holds tenure—almost total ownership of a job—and cannot be terminated without elaborate proceedings and objective proof of incompetence or misconduct. Further, in order to establish objective examinations and also to allow for equitable pay among comparable jobs,

28 Public Organization Behavior and Development

position classification systems were devised. By defining precisely the duties to be performed these systems also allow greater movement of employees into government and among jobs and agencies. As Van Riper has so aptly put it, "Work has been divided into segments capable of using interchangeable parts, so to speak."[13]

Most of the states and some cities followed the federal government's example, and by the 1930s the civil service philosophy generally characterized government employment. In 1938 President Roosevelt further entrenched the civil service philosophy by establishing personnel offices in each agency to implement and oversee the procedures of civil service employment. These offices were to be staffed by professional personnel workers—a measure that has further stabilized the approach and its attendant policies and procedures.

The civil service movement, the administrative management approach, and scientific management, while all contributing somewhat different elements to the form of public organizations as we know them today, also have some important elements in common

——They all represent in one way or another the predominant western applied philosophy of their day—that *rationality* and *efficiency* achieved through scientific methods and principles offer the solution to the need for more effective organizations.
——The focus was on the organizational structure and procedures with the assumption that employees should fit into their slots pretty much as interchangeable parts.
——In order to induce employees to adhere to the prescribed procedures, controls were exerted through a hierarchical "command system."
——Beliefs about employee motivation emphasized needs for security (protection from arbitrary firing) and economic goods (wages and incentives).

THE HUMAN RELATIONS MOVEMENT

All along good managers have known, however, that there is another side to the organization, a side that is less precisely described but equally important. This aspect is where *leadership*, as opposed to *administration,* seems to come into play, and it is referred to in the early management literature in vague terms like *esprit de corps.* Doubtless many successful managers were aware that behavior could not be totally controlled by rules and sanctions and that employees who felt good about themselves, their supervisor, their work unit, and their organization tended to follow the rules conscientiously and to do good work. Early in this century Mary Parker Follett, an organizational social scientist who was ahead of her time, advocated the need for *coordination* by means other than unilateral authority and also sensed the importance of group relationships.[14] However, it remained for Elton Mayo and F. J. Roethlisberger and their *Hawthorne studies* to popularize the impact of the human element in organizational setting.[15]

Beginning in the 1920s a series of field research projects were conducted at the Hawthorne Plant of the Western Electric Company in Chicago. Initially the project had a scientific management orientation—to study the effects upon worker productivity of such physical factors as the intensity of lighting, hours of work, and rest pauses. As the results began to unfold, however, there were some unanticipated trends. Productivity increased when the level of illumination was increased, but when illumination was then lowered to the original level, production continued to climb. It also climbed in a control group that had experienced no lighting change. These and other similar findings prompted the engineers who were conducting the studies to seek the assistance of Elton Mayo of the Graduate School of Business at Harvard.

Mayo's research team carried out more experiments on working conditions and productivity, developed techniques for observing and recording the interactions of members of work units, and conducted unstructured (nondirective) interviews with thousands of workers. The findings of these studies and the implications that Mayo and his colleagues drew from them described a view of the relationship between the worker and the organization that was quite different from the traditional picture. Many more factors than simply desire for security and economic rewards were seen to be operating. Furthermore, the social and organizational consequences of the earlier narrow views of the employee were now documented.

Mayo along with Roethlisberger and Dixon demonstrated, above all, the importance of the *human element* in organizations. In addition to the formal organization described by the traditional theorists there is an *informal* organization. It consists of the relationships of the employees as they function together in their work units. And it heavily influences how things are *really* done—as opposed to how they are supposed to be done. For example, informal work group norms (shared expectations) may offset an economic incentive system installed by management. Workers are motivated by social as well as economic factors.

Findings from the Hawthorne studies also highlighted the importance of feelings and attitudes. Workers who believed they were appreciated by management and listened to when they had reactions to working conditions were more productive. They were also more likely to feel committed to the organization and less likely to be in conflict with it. And the *Hawthorne effect*—the tendency for workers to raise their productivity simply because they receive attention and feel important—has become part of the language of management.

The writings of the Hawthorne researchers and others who followed them found fertile ground among management educators and the newly developing field of personnel administration. As the findings were translated into personnel programs and training sessions, the term *human relations* became a synonym for enlightened, people-oriented management. Finally, it was believed by some, the appropriate human element had been placed in the organizational performance equation. Unfortunately, the sense of closure was premature. This approach tended to commit the opposite fallacy of the traditional theories. Instead of organizations without people we now had people without organizations.

Perhaps because Mayo and his colleagues overinterpreted their findings, but mainly because a large number of followers were looking for nostrums and easy solutions (as were the stopwatch-toting efficiency experts who followed Taylor), human relations became a fad and a bag of tricks. Under the belief that satisfaction would lead to higher productivity, a plethora of fringe benefits, company newsletters, and human relations training programs were instituted. Psychologist J. A. C. Brown labeled these tactics cow psychology (contented cows presumably give more milk) and studies found the satisfaction-productivity belief to be in error.[16] Too many other factors influence employee productivity for there to be a predictable relationship. While in some studies there is indeed a positive correlation between morale and productivity, other studies show no correlation at all, and still others a negative relationship. So, the general findings of Mayo are still widely accepted as establishing the importance of human interaction processes in work, although the studies have recently been severely criticized by some. But the need for practical techniques for better dealing with the human side of the organization still persists.

The reader should be aware that while the Hawthorne researchers are exalted by some current scholars as the founders of the behavioral science of organizations, they are severely criticized by others. Recent reviews have accused Mayo and his colleagues of deliberately setting-out to demonstrate the importance of social variables, of interpreting the findings to fit their own values, and of omitting from their conclusions several important considerations such as the worsening depression in the 1930s, the influence of group incentives, the effects of participation and psychological conditioning, and of the invalid assumption that satisfaction and cohesiveness lead to productivity. H. M. Parsons has called the Hawthorne studies "the biggest Rorschach blot in the history of behavioral and social science." There is so much information and some of it is so subjective that it is possible to read into it any meaning one likes. At this point in time it is perhaps safest to say that the Hawthorne studies should receive recognition as bringing social variables to the awareness of managers and scholars, but that their specific conclusions are to be treated with care.[17]

APPLIED BEHAVIORAL SCIENCE

Even though the Hawthorne studies proved not to provide a panacea for all the human problems of organizations, they certainly helped lay much of the necessary groundwork for the necessary research on human behavior in organizations to continue. Scientists began spending a good deal of time studying agencies and firms, especially when World War II brought about the critical need to obtain high productivity in new or vastly expanded organizations. The Office of Naval Research and the U.S. Army have been sponsors of a large share of this research. This work is still going on among sociologists, social and organizational psychologists, anthropologists, educators, and other investigators. Although there is currently no single label for this field, the term *applied behavioral science* appears to have survived as well as any. Others are organizational behavior, industrial humanism, and human relations. This field is characterized by a dual commitment to ongoing research and to developing techniques for applying the findings to practical situations.

The field of applied behavioral science is now vastly expanded and diverse and includes industrial-organizational psychology and sociology, organization theory, applied anthropology, clinical psychology, adult education, and various administrative sciences. Indeed, a small fraction provides the basis for most of the rest of this book. We will briefly describe the general outlines of the field in order to provide you, the reader, an initial perspective of the field.

Students of organization use a variety of "levels of analyses" to study their subject. Some focus specifically and narrowly on a phenomenon such as communication channels. Others speculate more broadly on the place of the organization in modern society. An important level of analysis from our point of view is the *person*. For where else do the ideas, hopes, plans, and emotions that energize the agency exist but inside the individual? In a real sense the organization is an abstraction that exists largely in the minds of its members and observers. Without the *meanings* that are provided by the human minds, organizations are only piles of stone and metal and blobs of ink on pieces of paper.

One important subfield in individual psychology is the study of *motivation*, which is the area in which behavioral science is making a major contribution. We now have a more adequate (though still incomplete) picture of human drives and needs than did Weber and Taylor. Much more is involved than safety and money when an employee makes decisions about his or her commitment to the organization and its goals. The structure of the human need system, the impact of past experiences, the formation of expectations, and the way feelings are dealt with are pertinent to understanding employee behavior and thus significant to managers.

Other areas of individual organizational behavior include perception, learning, and problem solving. We humans are more than passive reservoirs of emotion. In spite of the current emphasis on feelings (useful because this aspect of ourselves has been underemphasized in the past) we do have other capacities that help us cope with the world. These include the abilities to gather accurate information through perception and communication, analyze the information, and take action.

From individual behavior the applied behavioral sciences move to the study of the interaction among people within groups and organizations. Employees as humans are social creatures. In this subfield, which I refer to as *process*, the need for translating knowledge about behavior to action becomes critical. The traditional theories, focused as they are on *structure*, often have little of value to say about how to improve behavioral processes such as communication and collaboration or how to resolve problems of conflict and competition—except to reorganize. The behavioral sciences are striving to devise explanatory models for understanding better the process variables and the skills necessary for dealing with them in real situations. When one purports to teach competency rather than just knowledge, traditional academic eyebrows are raised. But many applied behavioral scientists assert they have made a significant beginning in affecting interaction processes in useful ways.

The work of applied behavioral scientists moves to the total organization to attempt to apply what is known about individual behavior and process at the system level. Things at this stage become more complex. There are a number of organization theories—many stemming from the tradition of Weber and the administrative management theorists. However, many tend to be largely *descriptive*; that is, they aim to paint a picture of the organization as it functions. Unless one owns the organization and can move the boxes on the chart around at will, such approaches tend to stop short of providing much help to the operating manager or the consultant. There are some models and studies that are contributing to the field of *organization design*, a more prescriptive emphasis on changing organizational performance by redesigning the structural characteristics. For example, we are able to say some things about the characteristics of effective systems, about

34 Public Organization Behavior and Development

viable relationships between components of the organization, and about processes for improving employee satisfaction and productivity.

The study of leadership and management is a subfield that does not lack for prescriptive writing. Every leader, or follower, for that matter, seems to feel a unique insight into the dynamics of successful leadership. Successful leaders do not hesitate to share their views, and the advice does not fall on deaf ears. Our society places a high premium on achievement, power, and notoriety, and those who hope to find a formula for their own success are an eager market. Chester Barnard, corporation president and public administrator, made a significant impact on thinking about leadership in his *Functions of the Executive*.[18] Woodrow Wilson is considered to be one of the founders of the field of public administration because of an 1887 article in *Political Science Quarterly* entitled "The Study of Administration." And many other public figures set down their ideas prior to the modern trend for presidents and other leaders to write their memoirs. It is difficult, however, to put experiences and feelings into words in a form that makes them equally applicable to other people. Some insights about leadership that are based on more than individual experiences are now becoming available. Research studies, the analysis of the functioning of effective leaders and managers and psychological profiles of the successful, should prove useful to students and practicing managers alike.

The final aspect of this field is the most action-oriented aspect of the lot—that of planned change and organization development. We agree with whoever it was who said, "if you really want to understand something—try to change it." Public organizations are no exception to the general truth that contemporary organizations and institutions are very difficult to change in an intentional fashion. A special subfield of applied behavioral science has grown up in response to the problem of bringing about change. It is based on basic behavioral science knowledge but also includes a rapidly developing set of program methodologies and consultant and facilitator techniques and is burdened with a special set of value dilemmas.

All of these areas and levels of study, taken together, constitute the applied behavioral science of organizations. The basic issues and problems are much the same, probably, as they were for organizations in the ancient civilizations. As we trace the development of knowledge and organizations through the chapters that follow, we will see the topics below emerge again and again, sometimes in different forms, but always related to the utilization of human resources in organizational settings.

Goals

——What are the basic purposes or mission of the organization?
——What are the procedures whereby policies get formulated and/or changed?
——Do the members of the organization understand the goals and policies and do they accept them?

Authority

——Who is formally and officially in charge?
——How do those in charge obtain their power (election, ownership, physical strength, legislation, and so on)?
——What are the procedures whereby decisions get made and implemented?
——How, and in what ways, is authority divided, shared, delegated?
——How do followers or members feel about the authorities and the ways they use and share their authority?
——Are there unofficial, *informal* centers of power and leadership in the organization that may act against formal authority?

Organization: Structure and Tasks

——What are the major functions that need to be performed, and how is the organization to be divided up to perform them?
——Within each function what are the specific tasks that need to be performed?
——What specialized knowledge, skills, and characteristics are needed by the people who perform the needed tasks?

Organization: Rules, Procedures, Regulations

—What formal rules and procedures are necessary to assure appropriate task performance?
—What regulations are necessary to assure appropriate member nontask behavior (safety, cleanliness, timeliness, and so on)?
—How do members feel about and respond to these rules and regulations?
—In what manner, and with what degree of success, are these rules enforced?

Membership

—What needs and expectations do members have, and to what degree are these satisfied through their work?
—Do members feel supported and encouraged by the organization, or deserted and threatened?
—Is there morale and commitment to the organization?
—Are members able to learn, grow psychologically, and achieve more interesting and challenging work?

Cooperation

—Are the subunits and specialized personnel able to mesh their efforts to complement and assist one another?
—Is the quality of communication such that necessary information flows in a timely fashion, in all directions, by the most efficient path?
—Is conflict among people or units identified and resolved?

Information and Control Processes

—Is information necessary for making decisions and correcting problems gathered reliably and routed to appropriate points?
—Are ongoing operations monitored and evaluated effectively according to established standards?
—Is there a procedure for sensing environmental changes, new problems, and new opportunities?

Technology: Machines, Materials, Work Methods

—Is new technology being brought into the organization?
—What is the impact of this technology on the rest of the units?

Change: Temporariness in Roles, Structures, Tasks, Group Membership

—Is the organization undergoing internal or external changes that require adaptation and readjustment?
—Is the organization able to incorporate change smoothly, or is there resistance?
—Are there mechanisms (personnel, roles, units) that assist in change processes?

Interaction with Environment: External Social-Cultural-Political Forces

—What significant pressures, demands, and opportunities exist in the community or society outside the organization?
—What procedures does the organization have for developing responses to environmental influences?
—What significant values, concerns, and needs flow from the external world into the organization?
—What responsibilities does the organization have to respond to needs or problems in its environment?

CONCLUSION

The previous listing of some of the major issues and concerns of organizations should help make it clear why management is not an easy job and why the relationship between the individual and the organization is not always a smooth one. Actually, no organization operates like a well-oiled machine. In fact, the more one strives for such a condition in this day and age, the more the organization is pushed toward extinction. Decision making, problem solving, change, and response to crises are the order of the day. And, yet,

38 Public Organization Behavior and Development

as contemporary management theorist Bertram Gross has pointed out, when we take action to solve an organizational problem, we usually create another problem.

In order to provide an overall way of looking at and thinking about the phenomena we have described, theorists have utilized the concept *system*. By a system they mean a dynamic (ongoing and changing) body made up of interdependent parts. The catch phrase is: "Everything is related to everything else." You cannot take an action in one place without risking unanticipated consequences elsewhere. Like another of the more elegant systems, the human body, each subunit has its function, the state of one organ or subsystem affects the whole, and the whole system is no stronger or healthier than the weakest link.

From the perspective of human resource utilization it is useful to think of organizations as *sociotechnical systems*. Individuals and groups interact continually with technology (machinery, information processing devices, scientific techniques). The success of this interaction depends upon the ability to answer the questions and solve the problems we have listed in this section.

NOTES TO CHAPTER 2

1. I am indebted to C. S. George, *The History of Management Thought*, Englewood Cliffs, N.J.: Prentice-Hall, 1968, for much of the information in this section.
2. Robert Presthus, *Public Administration*, 6th ed., New York: Ronald Press, 1975, p. 185.
3. George, op. cit., p. 6.
4. Ibid., p. 13
5. Francis Cornford, *The Republic of Plato*, New York: Oxford University Press, 1959.
6. This summary of Weber's "ideal-typical" bureaucracy is adapted from Peter Blau, *Bureaucracy in Modern Society*, New York: Random House, 1956, Chapter 2.
7. Quoted in J. P. Mayer, *Max Weber and German Politics*, London: Faber, 1943, pp. 127-28.
8. Luther Gulick and Lyndall Urwick (eds.), *Papers on the Science of Administration*, New York: Institute of Public Administration, 1937.
9. Frederick W. Taylor, *Principles of Scientific Management*, New York: Harper, 1913.

10. For one of the most updated versions, see Herbert A. Simon, *Administrative Behavior: A Study of Decision-Making Organizations*, 3d ed., New York: The Free Press, 1976.

11. Saul W. Gellerman, *The Management of Human Resources*, Hinsdale, Ill.: Dryden Press-Holt, 1976.

12. See, for example, Leonard D. White, *The Federalists: A Study in Administrative History*, New York: Macmillan, 1956.

13. Paul P. Van Riper, "The Taproots of American Public Personnel Administration," *Personnel Administration*, vol. 25, March–April 1968, pp. 12–16, 32.

14. Henry C. Metcalf and Lyndall Urwick (eds.), *Dynamic Administration: The Collected Works of Mary Parker Follett*, New York: Harper & Row, 1940.

15. F. J. Roethlisberger, *Management and Morale*, Cambridge, Mass.: Harvard University Press, 1941. F. J. Roethlisberger and W. Dickson, *Management and the Worker*, Cambridge: Harvard University Press, 1956.

16. J. A. C. Brown, *The Social Psychology of Industry*, Baltimore: Penguin, 1954, p. 93.

17. H. McIlvane Parsons, "What Caused the Hawthorne Effect?", *Administration & Society*, volume 10, November 1978, pp. 258–283. Also see H. A. Landsberger, *Hawthorne Revisited*, Ithaca: Cornell University, 1958, and E. I. Cass and F. G. Zimmer (eds.), *Man and Work in Society*, New York: Van Nostrand Reinhold, 1975.

18. Chester Barnard, *The Functions of the Executive*, Cambridge, Mass.: Harvard University Press, 1938.

3

The Social Psychology of Work Behavior

In the field of public administration, interdisciplinary as it is, there is a controversy about what is the appropriate level of analysis. That is, what phenomena or processes should one focus on in attempting to understand and improve the functioning of organizational systems? Some would advocate the analysis of policy, others the study of structures and procedures. The viewpoint of this book, not surprisingly, is that human behavior is the place to begin.

In this chapter we will select from the growing literature on applied psychology a set of concepts and models that provides a succinct introduction to behavior in organizations. A caveat or two is necessary, however, before we begin. The field of applied psychology is at the point in its development at which it can provide fairly sound predictions about the behavior of people *in general* under specified circumstances. The prediction of the behavior of any specific individual is, however, riskier. We know, for example, that when most people find they have become the single deviant in a group they feel uncomfortable and bring their behavior back into line with the "norm." This does not hold true for everyone, however. A few stubbornly refuse to change and others become defiant. It is useful to know about group pressures for conformity, even though there are exceptions. It is also useful to know about deviants and the kinds of behaviors to expect from them.

Kurt Lewin, pioneer social psychologist, used the formula $B =$

$f(P + S)$ to explain the complexity of predicting human *behavior* (signified by B).[1] Behavior is a function f of the person (P)—everything the individual brings with himself or herself (memories, habits, skills, attitudes, emotions, and so on)—plus the *situation* (S)—all the many factors operating to influence behavior—such things as other people, tasks to be done, problems, messages, and resources. The possible interactions of all these personal and situational variables are numerous. Human behavior is more complex than some "pop" psychology books would have us believe, especially when we are trying to gain enough understanding to take some sort of action. But human behavior is not random, there is order to it, and it can be understood—although at a less than perfect probability of accuracy.

MANAGING BEHAVIOR IN ORGANIZATIONS

As we noted in the preceding chapter, the need to understand the behavior of employees has long been a concern of managers. "Getting things done through people" is one definition of the manager's role. An individual administrator can accomplish very little alone; it is the manager's ability to marshall the energies of others that makes the difference. And it is evident that except under conditions of absolute authority (slavery, military rule, threat of starvation, and so on), employees make decisions about whether to put forth their best efforts or just get by; whether to help the organization or sabotage it; whether to disclose important information or conceal it.

What conditions in the work environment are likely to bring about positive responses in the "average" employee? What managerial styles and skills are likely to lead to a productive relationship between supervisor and subordinate? And, finally, what broader *programs* of employee relations, training, and development are most likely to prevent or ease employee problems and lead to greater satisfaction, productivity, and growth? These are the significant questions.

The same questions can and should be asked from a slightly different angle. Important as it is to understand others, it is even more important that the manager understand himself or herself.

Do you, as a present or future manager, know what your strongest needs, goals, and values are? Do you know what kinds of situations and people are likely to elicit emotional responses from you, and why? Do you know your predominant leadership styles and skills? When you do poorly in dealing with certain situations do you know why and what you might do about it? Do you know how you feel about power and how you use it? The questions go on and on. There are no magic formulas for inspiring or motivating or manipulating people, but there are ways of behaving that increase the possibilities of success under given circumstances. While managerial success is unlikely to result from reading a book, it is possible through study to increase one's probabilities of success. Our discussion will follow the three basic subfields of psychology: emotion and motivation, perception, and learning.

HUMAN EMOTION AND MOTIVATION

The human organism is a system in which everything is related to everything else, including psychological processes. Thus there is no single aspect of behavior that provides an automatic beginning point for study. A single act of behavior is likely to involve all of the processes of emotion, motivation, perception, thinking, using past learnings, and so on. A good place to begin the study of work behavior is with the related topics of emotion and motivation.

For as long as humans have had the capacity to introspect and seek self-understanding, they have wondered about the energizing forces or drives underlying behavior. Why do people pursue the things they do? Why are there love and hate and fear? Why do some strive relentlessly to achieve wealth or power while others are content with less effort and fewer possessions? These questions have been asked throughout recorded history.

As thinkers have sought to explain the source and energy of human emotions they have suggested many possibilities. Primitive writings sometimes located the source of emotions outside the person—in spirits or demons who were in charge of such phenomena as love or greed or bravery. Others believed in instincts—a reservoir of inherited "programs" were thought to be in charge of various aspects of life. ("He has the *instincts* of a leader.")

Another common theme has been that emotions are the products of the clash of powerful internal forces, for example, Freud's *id* (biological-sexual drives) and *superego* (responsible social controls). Or the *hedonism* of the Greeks who perceived that humans expend their energy seeking pleasure and avoiding pain. And, of course, many religions incorporate motivation into their views about the contest between good and evil. Eastern religions and philosophies also have something to say about motivation. They see it as representing the ebb and flow of the forces of nature.

Similarly, views about work motivation have ranged widely. As we noted in the last chapter, theories of management have been based, in part, on assumptions about the nature of people—including their emotional and motivational systems. The assumption that the hedonistic model fit workers (but not management) was common. If one assumes that workers are by nature lazy and irresponsible and unmotivated to seek anything except selfish pleasure, one will arrange to run an organization in such a way as to override these deficits. Or, if one assumes that the seeking of economic rewards is a primary drive, then it follows that a management approach should utilize that principle. And if people are basically irrational, rationality needs to be imposed by management.

Before going into the current views of work motivation, it may be helpful to the reader who seeks a useful theory to discuss the study of motivation. Human motivation is an intangible entity— what scientists call a *construct*. Like electricity, we cannot see it, but can only observe its effects. Thus, we study the behavior of workers to see what they seem to want, what makes them work harder, what they complain about, and so on. From our observations we *infer* some things about the motivational systems of employees. Our theories of motivation, as a result, will depend partly on our basic orientation in psychology, as well as on the behaviors we choose to study and the kinds of questions we ask. They will also depend upon the people and work situations we observe, our notions of what we want to *do* with our theory, and a variety of other factors. Thus, the question of which view of motivation is best is extremely difficult to answer. In the study of work motivation we can at least consider these factors: (1) Does the theory overcome some of the obvious oversimplification of earlier theories? (2) Does it make sense to us—does it fit our experience? (3)

Is it useful, does it allow us to understand some things we didn't understand before? It will be helpful to keep these questions in mind as we review some of the current theories of work motivation.

There were few formal theories of work motivation until about the time of the Hawthorne studies—although there were, as we have said, plenty of assumptions about why people behave the way they do. Mayo and his followers are noteworthy because they demonstrated that the common assumptions were incomplete and some new elements needed to be added.[2] Specifically, workers did not conform to the assumptions of traditional theory but seemed to be affected in both their satisfaction and output by feelings or sentiments related to their work groups and supervisors. Clearly, a better understanding of this aspect of behavior was needed.

It is common to begin the discussion of modern theories of work motivation with the *need hierarchy* of Abraham Maslow.[3] Maslow was a clinical psychologist who became interested in those aspects of humans that extend beyond the lowest level of survival and materialistic needs. At the same time, he wanted a framework that would assume the fewest hereditary or inborn needs and allow a role for human maturation and learning. The hierarchy pictured in Figure 3-1 illustrates his model.

According to Maslow's formulation the inborn *physiological* needs form the foundation of the human need system. These needs include the basics of survival—food, water, warmth, reproduction, and so on. The needs are inherited, although the manner in which they are expressed may be learned.

If the physiological needs are well enough satisfied for survival, the organism, as it matures, develops needs for *safety* and *security*. These are learned responses that derive from the experiences of pain, being left alone, being dropped, and so on. If threats to safety have been severe and impactful they may persist as a predominant force throughout the individual's life.

If safety needs are well enough satisfied for development to continue a set of *social* or *affiliative* needs emerges. These needs are based on the fact that the individual has learned that other people are important because they frequently make the difference in regard to the satisfaction or frustration of other needs. Love, belonging, intimacy, and other variations of affiliative needs rep-

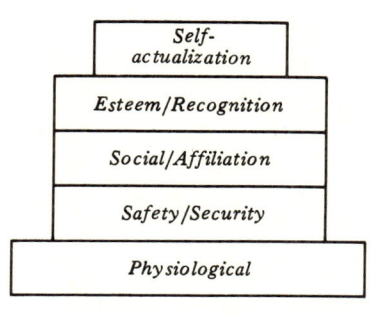

```
          ┌─────────────┐
          │    Self-    │
          │actualization│
      ┌───┴─────────────┴───┐
      │ Esteem/Recognition  │
   ┌──┴─────────────────────┴──┐
   │    Social/Affiliation     │
┌──┴───────────────────────────┴──┐
│        Safety/Security          │
├─────────────────────────────────┤
│         Physiological           │
└─────────────────────────────────┘
```

Figure 3-1 Maslow's Hierarchy of Needs

resent a crucial stage of development. Individuals who are able to satisfy these needs relatively well are able to move to the next level of motives. Those whose affiliative needs are unsatisfied are likely to have difficulty with relationships.

The next level, *esteem* and *recognition,* are often referred to as *ego* needs. At this stage the individual desires to differentiate himself or herself from the others to gain a sense of positive evaluation. Striving to excel, to achieve status, and to be recognized are symptoms of this need.

If all the other needs are satisfied, the individual may achieve *self-actualization.* This, the most advanced of the stages on Maslow's hierarchy, is expressed by fulfilling one's potential to develop or perform in particular areas. Things that are done for the enjoyment and stimulation of doing rather than because of needs at the other levels of the hierarchy are indicative of self-actualization.

The five categories of need differ in their relative strengths from one person to another and within the same person from one time to another. Basically, the strength of a need decreases when it is satisfied and increases when there is deprivation. The strength of a need tends to be higher overall in a person who has not experienced adequate satisfaction of that need in the past. For example, an individual who comes from a background of economic deprivation and insecurity is likely to have higher security needs than one from a comfortable background, and these are likely to remain strong for many years.

Maslow's model has been criticized on a number of counts. For some individuals the need levels may develop in a different order or simultaneously. Or a somewhat different set of categories may seem more useful. And the concept of self-actualization, which for Maslow was a relatively rare attainment, has been criticized. Nevertheless, the basic notion of a developing hierarchy of human needs based on interaction between heredity and learning is widely accepted.

Recently Clayton Alderfer has developed a research-based theory of motivation which is similar in some ways to Maslow's, but which is perhaps easier for managers to conceptualize and apply. Alderfer's categories of need are *existence, relatedness,* and *growth.*[4] Existence needs are those material and financial factors necessary for physical existence and comfort; relatedness needs are those pertaining to the establishment of affirming and supportive relationships with other people. Growth needs are those having to do with learning, creativity, and the attributes Maslow referred to as self-actualization. Alderfer conducted his research in organizational settings. The findings are complex because although each need area, if unsatisfied, leads to higher desire for that need, satisfaction of relatedness and growth needs does not quell the need, but leads to further desires in those needs areas. There are other findings which add further to the complexity, but for present purposes the Alderfer research confirms Maslow's assertion of the presence of strong needs in aspects of work outside the areas of survival and security.

Another popular motivational theorist is Frederick Herzberg, whose *two-factor theory* of work motivation has appealed to many managers.[5] Herzberg and his colleagues have utilized the critical incident interviewing technique to learn from workers and managers what kinds of work situations make them feel good about their jobs and what kinds make them feel bad. The data collected from large numbers of employees at all levels in various kinds of organizations form a fairly stable pattern of *satisfiers* and *dissatisfiers*. Herzberg's findings are summarized in Table 3-1. The interesting discovery is that dissatisfaction tends to be caused by a different class of factors than those causing satisfaction—they are not the opposites of each other. Factors said to cause dissatisfaction are *hygiene* factors in Herzberg's terms. They are largely situational characteristics such as working conditions, pay, and

Table 3-1 Work Motivation Incentives

Hygiene factors (extrinsic)	Motivator factors (intrinsic)
Company policy and administration	Achievement
Supervision	Recognition
Wages	Work itself
Interpersonal relations	Responsibility
Working conditions	Advancement
	Growth

Adapted from Frederick Herzberg, "One More Time: How Do You Motivate Employees?", *Harvard Business Review*, January-February 1968, p. 57.

organizational policies. The *motivators,* on the other hand, are more closely related to the work itself and have to do with achievement, recognition, and challenging work.

Herzberg's research has been retested (or "replicated") numerous times. The results are usually, but not always, the same—demonstrating our earlier point about the imperfection of research findings. In some situations there seems to be some "cross over" of factors. That is, pay may be mentioned more frequently as a motivator or lack of interesting work as a dissatisfier than Herzberg's studies showed. The model may fit some occupational or class groups better than others, or work motives may vary according to one's history of work security or other factors.

Although the theories of Maslow, Alderfer, and Herzberg are not interchangeable (they are based on different methods and focuses), they do provide a fairly consistent and mutually reinforcing view of human motivation as applied to work. And they provide the manager with some solid clues about how to better understand employees and about how to arrange the work environment to maximize satisfaction. More particularly, we know the range of human motives or needs, something about the variations in level and intensity of motivation, and a good deal about the conditions of the work environment that will probably affect these needs. One problem with the research and theorizing on human motives is that the relationship between need satisfaction and productivity is not clearcut. Raising the satisfaction level does not necessarily raise productivity, although it usually reduces absenteeism and turnover. One approach for dealing with this problem as well as providing a more operational approach to work motivation is *expectancy theory.*

Nadler, Hackman, and Lawler, proponents of expectancy theory, point out that managers have difficulty utilizing the newer behavioral science views of work motivation because they do not allow for differences in motives among employees, nor do they account for situational differences.[6] Neither do they allow for the fact that employees participate actively in the motivational process by making decisions about how to behave, based on *expectancies* of what kind of behavior will lead to a desired outcome. Thus an employee who desires maximum financial reward (because of the state of his or her need system) and believes that working very hard will lead to that outcome can be expected to work hard. Another employee who wants financial reward but feels that politicking is most likely to lead to the goal will behave accordingly. Similarly, an employee whose predominant needs are for security and safety will function so as to minimize risk rather than maximize productivity and will seek to settle into a secure position that would be unsatisfactory to someone whose needs for status are high.

An additional factor is that employees are likely to choose behaviors that they believe they can perform successfully. Thus, an employee whose need system is such that she places a premium on close and supportive social relationships at work might consider several alternative strategies. Her decision would be heavily influenced by her sense of which one she could implement most successfully—for example, seeking a job in an office where a close friend works as opposed to attempting to actively build a support group with strangers.

Nadler and Lawler propose the following diagnostic procedure for managers who want to develop a strategy for improving worker productivity.[7]

1. Find out what outcomes each employee desires. This can be done by utilizing the theories of motivation discussed earlier, in conjunction with observation of workers' behavior and interviews. Also, questionnaires have been devised for this purpose.

2. Establish your own definition of the performance you are seeking. One frequent difficulty is that managers have not established clearly with themselves and their employees objective criteria for the productivity they want. This is one of the reasons for the popularity of management by objectives and other goal-setting exercises.
3. Make sure that expected kinds and levels of performance are attainable by the employees and are so perceived by them. Otherwise motivation will be low.
4. Make clear and explicit behavioral links between employees' desired outcomes and your desired productivity. Establish a procedure whereby the employee can attain his or her goals by attaining the kind and level of performance you have decided is important for your unit's success. This may require redesign of the job and/or changing the external rewards. For example, if the employee values achievement, it is important to create a work situation in which high performance will lead to such things as increased responsibility and challenge. Nadler and Lawler point out that it is crucial to check out with the employee the adequacy of the reward system *in his or her view.* The employee's perception of reality, not the manager's, is crucial.
5. Make sure there are not subtle conflicting expectancies in the situation. Other factors independent of the manager's reward system may interfere. One example is negative outcomes of desired performance—such as employees being criticized by others for working hard and threatening the lesser producers. Another example would be an organization procedure that forced high producers to take on increased loads.
6. Make sure rewards for performance are perceived by employees as large enough to motivate them, rather than as token or trivial.
7. Check the strategy to make sure that it does not cause inequities. Under this system there may well be *differences* among employees' reward systems, but it is important that they not be perceived as unfair.

There are several implications of the expectancy model that are important for organizational policies and design. We will explore these at a later point. At this stage several problems, or at least reservations, about the model need to be pointed out. One is that if pursued in its pure form, a separate reward system for each employee would need to be devised. This may not be possible because of a variety of situational constraints. Thus, some compromise between providing one reward system for everyone (an obvious error) and a separate one for each employee may have to be discovered.

Another problem with the model is that employees' needs may change. We have already indicated that for some people, some needs once met are no longer dominant. Thus, the manager who utilizes the expectancy model should be prepared for the likelihood that some employees' reward systems may have to be changed from time to time.

A third problem with the model is that in some cases it may turn out that an employee's needs are simply not compatible with the potential rewards of a position. For example, an employee may have high needs for achievement but skills inadequate to bring about such achievement in a given job. In this case alternatives such as additional training or transfer to another position may be necessary.

Fourth, in a government organization with an established civil service system, the manager likely does not have control over many of the reward factors, including pay, promotion, task, or working conditions. Thus the manager's ability to manipulate the reward system is reduced.

In some respects, expectancy theory, like many other behavioral science models, seems like little more than common sense. However, it has the advantage of allowing for the utilization of the considerable body of research on motivation and is itself backed up by more than fifty studies. It is a significant advance over the assumption of pure economic motivation and the simplistic strategy of providing the same reward system for everyone.

OTHER EMOTIONAL-MOTIVATIONAL FACTORS

So far we have concentrated largely on the motivational forces that have directly to do with job performance and job satisfaction. It should be obvious that there are many other facets of the workers' experience in the organization that are not dealt with in such a discussion. We will consider some of the more significant of these emotional issues before proceeding on to other areas of the psychology of the worker.

ATTITUDES AND VALUES

In addition to their work-related motives, employees carry with them attitudes about many other facets of their environments. These attitudes may cause them to have strong emotional responses in particular situations. An employee who has strong attitudes in favor of formal, authoritative, structured supervision is likely to respond negatively to a supervisor who is democratic and informal. A male employee who holds a strong attitude that women are too unstable to make good managers will have problems when assigned to a female supervisor. Attitudes about people and events in the work environment interact with work motives to produce the employee's overall reaction to his or her position.

Attitudes are tricky to deal with because individuals may intentionally or unintentionally mask one attitude with another. Interviewers in the Hawthorne studies found, for example, that some workers voiced complaints about such things as the food in the cafeteria when the basic factors that were bothering them were concerns about where they stood with their supervisors and whether they were progressing within the organization. Thus, when strong attitudes are expressed the manager can be sure that something of emotional significance is going on. Just what the root is may take further exploration.

Attitudes are derived from our past experiences about which things are positive and rewarding and which are negative and punishing. They are also affected by our values—those things we believe about what is good or bad, right or wrong. Values are derived from the culture in which people live and from their more immediate families and acquaintances. These basic values affect our attitudes about working and also our work motivation. Some of the basic values are:

——Is it good and desirable to work industriously or is hard work pointless?

—Is it desirable to respect and obey those in positions of authority or should authorities be carefully evaluated before they are obeyed to be sure they are competent?
—Should individual employees subjugate their own needs and self-interests for the good of the organization, or is the purpose of the organization to respond to members' needs?
—Is competing rigorously and winning by whatever means necessary before others beat you the best strategy?
—Is the expression of anger and hostility to be avoided whenever possible?
—Is working for a public agency a stimulating and motivating opportunity to serve others or is it an avenue to a safe, secure, and unstressful job?

These are questions which, in an antiseptic scientific sense, have no answers. They involve *shoulds* and *oughts* and *goods* and *bads,* which depend on one's values.

The thing to remember about basic values and attitudes (as opposed to relatively superficial ones like which brand of toothpaste is best) is that those holding them usually strongly believe that they are accurate pictures of the world. They are difficult to change through rational argument and intense emotion may be aroused if they are violated.

STRESS

Sometimes individuals hold attitudes and values detrimental to their mental or physical health. An individual with a basic antipathy toward authority gets crosswise with every supervisor he works for, and each confrontation reinforces his view that administrators are power mongers and not to be trusted. Another individual believes her entire worth as a person depends upon her ability to excel and produce more than anyone else. She overworks, ignoring the signs of stress in her own body, until her health is adversely affected. Still another has been taught that other people's feelings are more important than his own and that he should withhold the expression of any negative expression in order to avoid making other people feel bad. He lets others at work take advantage of him and does not tell them how angry he feels. Sometimes, however, he explodes at a seemingly innocuous statement and yells at the poor violator who wonders if the usually unassuming person isn't a little unstable after all.

These are all examples of what psychologists have traditionally called *neurotic* behavior. They are self-defeating behaviors in that the individual does not act in his or her best interests, allowing self-destructive attitudes or values to be in control. To the individual holding them, these attitudes and values are a part of his or her basic orientation to the world. People are often not clearly aware of their own attitudes. Further, they often do not perceive that changing them is a reasonable possibility.

Much of today's popular psychology consists of models to help the individual understand his or her own behavior and to identify and change self-limiting or self-damaging attitudes. Transactional Analysis is a way of describing behavior, and many people have found it useful because it utilizes straightforward descriptive language rather than the obscure jargon of some fields of clinical practice. It was developed by the late psychiatrist Eric Berne to help people improve their dealings with each other.[8] Each of us has three major aspects to our personality: the *parent* aspect is the set of attitudes and values which we derived from authority figures when we were younger. These are the prescriptions we carry around within us—how we and others "ought" to behave, how the world "ought" to be. When the parent aspect is strong, the individual is likely to rigidly impose many rules and demands on self and others, regardless of the realities of the situation.

The *child* aspect, on the other hand, represents the more spontaneous, self-oriented, unregulated part of each of us. When the child aspect is in control, the individual responds more to his or her own needs and feelings and often less responsible toward others. In life the parent and child aspects may have both positive and negative consequences. The parent aspect is a positive influence when the situation calls for control, responsibility, and rules. When it is appropriate to be free, spontaneous, and responsive to our needs, the child aspect is functional.

The third aspect, the *adult,* is the most objective and rational mode. The mature adult can look at each situation anew, gather as much information as possible, weigh the alternatives, and make a rational decision uncontaminated by old and irrelevant prescriptions or momentary emotions. The healthy individual can operate from any one of the three aspects when they are appropriate to the situation, rather than being bound to any one of them.

Berne and his followers have provided a useful approach to helping people overcome dysfunctional responses to situations. The manager, for example, who is overly prescriptive, controlling, and rule-oriented, may learn that she has developed from early experience an overly strong "parent", a part of which is so overly controlling that many subordinates feel stifled. In another situation an employee as a strong and rebellious "child" may react so negatively to authority that he is in continuous conflict with the supervisor and unable to work satisfactorily.

Albert Ellis, in his *rational-emotive therapy,* emphasizes that dysfunctional attitudes and values are often perpetuated in an individual's internal dialogue.[9] Neurotic behavior in Ellis's terms is doing things to yourself that block your effective functioning and make you anxious or unhappy. It basically has to do with the ways you think about problems and talk to yourself about them in negative, self destructive, and tension producing terms. An individual whose behavior is characterized by a fear of failure engages in self-talk which says, "It will be awful if I don't succeed. Failure is a terrible thing. I'll be ridiculed and made miserable, I won't be able to stand it!" The more the self-talk continues the more emotion the individual generates about the issue and the harder it is to perceive the trap one is caught in. Ellis's prescription is to help the individual identify the damaging attitudes or values (sometimes they operate below conscious awareness) and then challenge and replace them with less dire and more rational statements. "It will be unfortunate if I fail, but it won't be the first time and I'll no doubt recover quite well. No sense upsetting myself."

Thus far we have been discussing the stress that comes primarily from internal dynamics. Stress also can arise from external factors in the work situation. Because of its high cost in lost productivity, health care, and human discomfort, there has been a good deal of research done on sources of stress in the work situation. A study by French and Caplan on employees of federal agencies identified several organizational sources of stress.[10] These included work overload, role conflict, role ambiguity, conflicts in relationships with other units, poor interpersonal relationships, and lack of participation in decisions affecting one's life. It may be useful to provide further explanations of these stressors.

——Work overload pertains to the employees' perception that there is too much work to do in too little time.
——Role conflict occurs when the individual's job requires him or her to play several different roles which are not compatible.
——Role ambiguity, on the other hand, refers to unclear expectations and standards—not knowing what is expected or how one is to be evaluated.
——Conflicts with other units means that working relationships are strained and ineffective.
——Poor interpersonal relationships with co-workers lead to feelings of alienation, lack of support, and tension in getting collaborative tasks done.
——Lack of participation allows the individual less opportunity to influence factors in work that affect him or her and may lead to feelings of powerlessness.

Adams reports studies in which he found the above conditions to be related to chronic health problems and feelings of ineffectiveness and dissatisfaction.[11] It is important to note that it is not just the absolute amount of the factors, which if exceeded results in stress, but the individual's expectations about what is reasonable and desirable. The stressed individual is likely to be the one who is experiencing more demands or pressures than he or she can accept. Again, the expectancy principle operates to modify psychological reactions to external factors.

It behooves a manager to gain as much understanding as possible of the dynamics of stress in order to manage his or her own internal stresses and minimize the situational pressures on employees. It is beyond the scope of this book to prescribe programs for stress management, but a number of useful treatments are available.[12]

EMOTIONAL STYLES

Before leaving the topic of motivation it may be useful to acknowledge the significant organizational impact of *individual differences* in the kinds of emotions people experience and their unique ways of dealing with them. We have already noted that employees vary in regard to which of their needs are predominant at any given time. Clearly such differences, if they exist within a work group, can cause conflict. One employee who is functioning at the level of survival and security and another whose major motives are for status and recognition are unlikely to have compatible notions of how things should be done.

People also vary in their styles of expressing their feelings in dealings with others. Richard Wallen provided an illustration of these differences in his three types of *executive personality*.[13] He described the types as the *modest helper*, the *strong achiever*, and the *detached critic*. Each of these is categorized by different ways in which managers handle the basic emotions of tenderness and toughness.

Modest helpers avoid aggressive impulses and emphasize affection and good will. These types get things done by being helpful and building harmony. They are usually not good at dealing with conflict or standing firm.

Strong achievers function in the opposite manner. They reject tender and nurturing emotions and emphasize strength and toughness. Managers with this style accomplish their goals by being competitive and confronting. They are often not adept at dealing with relationship issues, negotiating, or operating in teamwork situations.

Detached critics reject both emotional extremes and attempt to stay cool, rational, and detached. They accomplish their work through analysis and logic rather than through persuading people or building emotional support. They are frequently poor at dealing with emotional issues.

The definitions are of pure types for the sake of illustration; no individual falls totally into a single category. Some combination of styles is probably best for most managerial situations. In our present discussion the listing of the types is meant to illustrate how emotional characteristics affect behavior.

Another concept, based on similar basic principles, is the concept of *androgyny* developed by Sandra Bem.[14] She notes that managers who emphasize the tough, assertive modes in their roles exemplify what we have traditionally viewed in the culture as *masculine* behavior. The nurturing, relationship-oriented mode is thought of as *feminine*. Some men and women get locked into these role stereotypes, assuming that it is inappropriate for men to be tender and nurturing or for women to be tough and assertive. There is, in fact, growing indication that an androgynous stance—a combination of both styles—is more mentally healthy and managerially effective.[15]

There are many other conceptions of differences in emotional styles, introvert-extrovert, OK–Not OK, and so on. Often emotional styles are very ingrained and difficult to change. Differences in style among those who work together can be sources of conflict and stress and can rarely be resolved by admonishing someone to "try to be a little more understanding," or "don't get mad so easily."

There is, as far as I know, little solid evidence of any pervading emotional differences between employees of public and private organizations. There is a fairly common belief that public employees are more concerned about safety and security than are employees in private organizations. This is presumably true because individuals with high needs for security are likely to seek employment in an organization with a seniority-oriented civil service system. There is also the possibility that working in a security-oriented system may affect employees' feelings about such conditions. In any event, any global differences between public and private employees are of only academic concern to the individual manager. The important point is to gain an understanding of the predominant needs, emotional styles, and stress points of those in the unit, including the manager himself or herself, and then dealing with these factors as openly and directly as possible, utilizing the Nadler and Lawler expectancy model or a similar diagnostic and problem-solving approach. There is no claim that such an approach is easy or that it provides sure-fire solutions to every employee relations problem. But in the long run it should prove more sound than formulas based on the assumption that everyone is alike and that a single solution is feasible.

PERCEPTION

Another important aspect of behavior has to do with the processes and mechanisms whereby we gather information from our environment. We have referred to this process in our earlier discussions,

58 Public Organization Behavior and Development

since behavior almost always includes perception, but there are some aspects of perception that are useful to managers and are thus worth noting. The study of perception includes, but is by no means limited to, the organs of the five senses and the acuity with which they pick up stimuli and transfer them to the central nervous system. There are elements of employees' performance that do involve these basic senses, adequacy of lighting, the noise level in work locations, and so on. Our focus here, however, will be on the impact of perceptual phenomena on the general behavior of employees.

EMOTIONAL PERCEPTION

An important transitional point between our discussions of emotions and perception is that the two are strongly related. In fact, it is an established psychological fact that emotions strongly affect what we perceive. Most of us assume that what we hear and see is fact—that it is the true picture of the world out there. However, we each perceive uniquely with our emotional, learning, and perceptual subsystems in interaction with our physiologies. Psychology journals of two decades ago were full of studies demonstrating this principle. Such studies are well reported in psychology texts and will not be reviewed here. It is easy to believe a study that shows that poor children remember coins to be larger than do other children, but it is more difficult, when sitting in a meeting, to hear four entirely different perceptions of a problem situation and to acknowledge calmly and accept the fact that the others are not blind or stupid, but are having their perceptions colored by their needs, allegiances, expectations, and other emotionally related factors. It is even harder to acknowledge the probability that even our own perceptions may be distorted on rare occasions!

There are certain conditions under which perceptual distortion is most likely to occur. The more ambiguous the situation the more likely perceptions will be distorted. (The Rorschach ink blot test is a completely ambiguous picture onto which the subject must project all of its meaning in order to perceive anything at all.) Beyond that, we tend to perceive those elements of a situation which we expect to be positive and need satisfying, to twist those things that are not so that they are more to our liking, and to ignore those things that are completely negative and need-frustrating. Group pressures can bring about perceptual distortions, as can strong values or political beliefs. Distortions can be minimized by reducing the level of threat and need for defensiveness in a situation. They can also be minimized by developing a climate in which first impressions are made on a tentative basis and checked out with others before final conclusions are reached.

SELF-PERCEPTIONS AND PERCEPTIONS OF US BY OTHERS

An important element of the perception-emotion dynamic has to do with how we see ourselves and how we want others to see us. Many psychologists believe that *self-image* represents one of the most central aspects of our psychological life. We each carry around a mental picture of ourselves as we would like to be seen, and we behave in ways that we believe will project this desirable image. We may wish, for example, to be seen as wise, strong, and brave. If we're normal we may harbor a few secret fears that perhaps we're not quite that way, or that even if we are others may not perceive us that way. So we may play-act, or wear a mask, to increase the chances of being seen in the way we wish to be. For example, we may pretend to know about a topic even though we are uninformed. One of the problems with this type of behavior is that it creates *incongruities* between what is going on inside us and what is being presented on the surface. These incongruities often cause emotional stresses if true feelings are repressed or camouflaged. They are also seen through by others much more often than we realize.

Because of the strong need to maintain their self-image, most people become defensive when disconfirming information is provided to them. We become angry when criticized. We rationalize when we get negative feedback in a performance appraisal interview. Or we assert that the test we took isn't valid and doesn't measure anything anyway. This is another reason why the logical-rational view of behavior in organizations is imperfect. People too frequently don't want or can't take information that is threatening to their self-image or other aspects of their basic psychology. In

60   Public Organization Behavior and Development

order for employees to learn more about their behavior and its impact on performance and on other people, the manager needs to work to minimize defensiveness and the need for self-protection in the work unit.

OTHER PROBLEMS IN PERCEPTION

In addition to the aspects of perception we have discussed thus far, there are numbers of other ways in which perception affects the process of administration. Zalkind and Costello summarized some of the important research on factors affecting the accuracy of a person's perceptions of other people.[16]

Forming Impressions of Others

——Stereotyping—making judgments about an individual based on his or her membership in ethnic, racial, vocational group.
——Halo effect—one predominant trait is used to evaluate someone, while other possibly contradictory evidence is overlooked. ("She has an outstanding attendance record, therefore, she must be a highly valuable employee.")
——Projection—ascribing our own feelings or characteristics to other people. (A person whose nature is to be angry and hostile may tend to perceive other people as hostile.)
——Perceptual defense—people are known to "put on blinders" in order to avoid being affected by threatening or distasteful people or events. (Managers who feel awkward or inept in dealing with an employee's problem behaviors may tend not to see those behaviors.)

Characteristics of the Perceivers

——Self-awareness and self-acceptance—People who know and accept themselves are more likely to perceive others accurately.
——Skills—accurate perception of others appears to be a combination of skills, including sensitivity to individual differences and norms.

Characteristics of the Perceived

——Status and role—a person's status in the organization and membership in certain groups may affect how he or she is perceived. For example, a member of top management may be perceived more knowledgeable, even about things unrelated to the organization.
——Visibility of traits—People who display their traits and characteristics more openly are easier to perceive accurately than those who are closed.

Situational Influences on Perception

——Group friendliness and congeniality—People tend to perceive others in a friendly group as more similar and compatible with themselves.
——Hierarchical role—Members often perceive people and units at their own level in the organization more accurately than those at other levels.

Zalkind and Costello's summary provides a number of clues to the administrator about sources of perceptual distortion to be on the lookout for. One obvious generalization is that we filter our perceptions of other people through our own feelings, biases, traits, and positions, and these filters have an impact on our views of the situation.

LEARNING, DEVELOPMENT, AND PROBLEM SOLVING

Some of the earliest contributions of the behavioral sciences to organizations were in the area of learning. Intelligence tests were first used on a large scale for selection purposes by the military forces in World War I. Tests for mechanical aptitude, clerical skills, and other capabilities to learn and perform have long been common in public organizations. But the emphasis shifted to the emotional-motivational area for reasons we discussed earlier and is only now moving back to include the rational, thinking side of human behavior. The Nadler and Lawler expectancy model that we discussed in the first part of this chapter is a good example of the new view. It asks the manager to use a rational analysis to diagnose work situations and develop strategies for action. The purpose of this section is to point out some of the ways in which human learning is significant for dealing with behavior in organizations.

Abilities

For reasons that we still do not fully understand, humans vary widely in their abilities to learn and perform many different tasks. Probably these individual differences are a result of the interaction of a number of factors including heredity, learning opportunities, motivation, health, and emotional stresses. Selection offices in organizations use various screening devices such as tests, interviews, work simulations, and evaluations of past performances to try to identify those candidates whose abilities best match the demands of the job. This square peg in the square hole approach has come under criticism from a number of fronts. Representatives of minority and disadvantaged groups have asserted that tests discriminate against candidates with fewer verbal and test-taking skills, even though they are fully capable of performing the job. Others feel selection methods take too static a view of human abilities, failing to allow for continuing learning and development. And still others point out that most humans perform up to only a small percentage of their full potential anyway, and that motivation and actualization are more important than abilities.

Even though differences in ability are probably not as fixed as previously supposed, they are still important in placing limits on performance. A consultant who works mostly with business executives told me that one of his most common and difficult tasks is to help clients acknowledge and respond to the individual differences in ability and style among their subordinates. Treating everyone alike (as opposed to treating them equitably) is not a sound strategy, nor is expecting them to react similarly to a request or a piece of information.

Basic Principles of Learning

Psychologists have been studying the process of learning for many years. The principles uncovered are more clearcut in controlled laboratory and classroom situations than in day-to-day organizational life, but there are some useful generalizations.

Some learning takes place because experiences happen *to* people. We got burned on a stove when we were very young (to use a stock example) and learned the meaning of the word *hot*. Or we may get a strong compliment from our boss for the way we wrote a report and learn to be sure to do it that way again. In this kind of learning, which helps us adapt to our environment, we tend to repeat those behaviors that lead to positive or rewarding experiences. We also tend not to repeat behaviors that lead to unpleasant or unsatisfying experiences. This process is often referred to as *conditioning*. Thus, there is a close link between learning and motivation.

Psychologist B. F. Skinner has gained notoriety for applying to human behavior the principles of learning derived from laboratory animal studies. His book *Beyond Freedom and Dignity* caused a stir because of his assertion that our behavior is shaped totally by the experiences we have beginning with birth.[17] In Skinner's view the learning process is directly linked to stimuli from the world in which we live, and we are, in a sense, captives of our experience. In seeking applications to human problems, Skinner's approach stresses positive rewards or "reinforcement." Behaviorism, as Skinner's approach is called, is being tried in work organizations. Pay and other incentives are used in a carefully scheduled program designed to improve performance. Immediate feedback and rewards for accomplishment are basic elements.

Skinner's work has been criticized by behavioral scientists with humanistic values because it takes a mechanistic view of human existence and advocates direct manipulation of behavior. Other criticisms dealing with the practicality and feasibility have also been voiced. Nevertheless, most observers agree that whether or not one accepts Skinner's philosophy, the principles of behavior modification he demonstrated bear serious consideration in employee incentive or training programs.

Real rewards (as opposed to cheap and indiscriminate praise) are effective incentives for encouraging learning and improving performance. It follows that one of the faults with some attempts to bring about employee learning (such as safety training programs or telephone manners campaigns) is that there are no clear-cut rewards or incentives associated with the learning and change being asked for. There are only vague and far-off threats of punishment, which leads to the next application issue.

There are several problems with using threats or punishment to bring about learning in organizations. One is that punishment often communicates only what was done wrong, not how to do it right. Penalizing workers through an incentive system when their productivity drops is an ineffective way to bring about learning unless instruction is provided about how to perform successfully. Another problem is that often punishment is only possible, not certain, and is off in the future. Drivers do not learn to drive within the speed limit and overweight persons continue to consume too many calories because the penalty is not certain, immediate, and significant.

Learning does not take place very effectively unless the learner finds out the results of his or her actions. The student who never finds out how he or she performed on an exam cannot learn until the *feedback loop* is completed, that is, until results of performance are fed back to the initiator. Learning programs that do not contain a feedback loop to let the learners know about the results of their actions ignore an important element of the learning process.

Another category of learning refers to situations in which the individual intentionally sets out to acquire a new skill or body of knowledge. Research by Alan Tough indicates that most adults do, in fact, invest considerable time and energy in their own learning if they are motivated to do so.[18] This is, if they perceive that the learning will provide something they desire. Interestingly, much of the energy of the organizational trainer goes into attempting to find ways to motivate trainees to learn. The fact of the matter is that most people do not have to be motivated by outside factors (in fact, cannot be) but are fully capable of being self-motivated if the reward system is adequate.

Much of the intentional, self-directed learning that adults engage in falls into the special category of *problem solving*. Problem solving utilizes the logical-rational side of the human behavior. It emphasizes the behaviors that traditional management theorists believed to be important: rationality, logic, and specific rules and procedures.

One approach to solving problems is, of course, trial and error.

Those who utilize this common technique (and that includes most of us at least part of the time) try a variety of solutions until one works. We hope that learning takes place over time and that we are able to improve our performance without a lot of conscious effort. However, since time delays and mistakes can be costly, there is usually motivation to improve upon the trial-and-error approach in organizations.

Although there are a variety of different problem-solving formulas, most of them have in common an approach to mental discipline through a series of steps. For example, (1) define the problem, (2) analyze the problem to determine its causes, (3) identify the possible alternative solutions, (4) weigh the alternate solutions, (5) select a solution and implement it, (6) evaluate the choice and begin the process again, if necessary. Such problem-solving behavior involves a higher order of mental process than does conditioning, may require rigorous training, and often is performed by groups as well as individuals.

Some administrative theorists have ascribed decision making (one version of problem solving) a central role in their pictures of the organization. Herbert Simon, Frederick March, and R. M. Cyert see administration as a process of making choices that lead to action. Decisions that are rational, which take account of the objective aspects of the situation, lead to greatest effectiveness. In this approach learning and skill development are crucial. So is the augmentation of the thinking process with sophisticated decision-making strategies and computer-based information-processing techniques.[19]

LEARNING: INTENTIONAL AND ACCIDENTAL

Because people do not always come to their positions with all the abilities they need, and because job demands and technologies change, it becomes important to provide for learning to occur. Training, whether offered in formal programs or on the job, is the organization's opportunity to influence the abilities and sometimes the attitudes and perceptions of employees. Some managers operate under the mistaken belief that training occurs only when someone plans and performs a formal program. Actually, training of an informal nature is occurring all the time the employee is in the organization. Each reward or punishment, each new procedure, each performance appraisal interview, each formal or informal communication contributes to learning. The problem is, of course, that while some learning is intentionally brought about and helpful to the organization, other learning is informal and accidental and may have a negative impact on productivity. In addition to learning correct procedures, new technologies, and leadership skills, employees may also be learning how much they can get away with, how to "psych out" the boss, what the organization *really* values as opposed to what it says are its goals, and how to manipulate and maneuver within the system.

It is the recognition that it is risky to leave learning to chance or to a hit-or-miss collection of short courses that has led observers such as Schon to propose the concept of the *learning system*.[20] His view is that any organization, but especially those involved in new and changing fields, needs to make ongoing and intentional learning for all members a formal and significant part of its business. The long-term health of the organization is closely tied to members' abilities to keep up with new professional and technical developments and to gain and sharpen their organizational skills. Some such skills can be though of as individual matters—how to perform an analysis, write a report, conduct an interview, and so on. Others are group- or system-level functions such as teamwork, meshing the efforts of several units, negotiating, and problem solving. These are increasingly being taught in formats such as *organization development* which utilize group-oriented training. The crucial point is that since the organization relies on the continuing development and updating of its members, it must assume a part of the responsibility for fostering a climate that is supportive of ongoing learning.

ADULT LEARNING AND CAREER DEVELOPMENT

Recent emphasis on learning as an integral part of organization life, as opposed to something that ends with one's formal attendance at high school or college, has fostered some useful new understandings of the learning dynamics of adults. Malcolm Knowles, pioneer in the field of adult learning, adopted the term *androgyny* to emphasize the fact that traditional education (pedagogy) refers to the teaching of children, and that adults learn best in somewhat different ways.[21] In one of his writings, Knowles identifies four assumptions about adult learning that differ from traditional pedagogy

1. As individuals mature psychologically they become less dependent on others and more able to be self-directing. This means that adults are ready to take more responsibility for their own learning, and that resentment about being treated like a child by being overcontrolled interferes with learning.
2. Adults bring to the classroom many more life experiences than do children, and these experiences play a major role in helping the adult define who he or she is. Educational programs that allow adults to contribute their experiences and to continue learning through *experiential* modes (discussions, projects, simulations, laboratories, and so on) provide opportunities to broaden and integrate learning.
3. Children are motivated to learn because others decide what they need to learn and establish academic incentives (grades, diplomas, and so on). Adults are motivated differently. Often their "readiness" for learning stems from a need to know based on problems and opportunities they encounter in their lives.
4. Pedagogy is subject-centered, and is based more on what one needs to know to pass a test, cope with the next course, get into college, and so forth. Hopes of application are delayed until "when you grow up" or "when you are in college." Adults tend to be problem-centered; they respond to material that is immediately pertinent to the solution of life issues and problems. The admonition that "someday this information will be useful to you" makes less sense to them.

Since organizational training programs are adult education operations, the pertinence of Knowles's ideas is obvious. They clearly add a view of human learning that extends beyond the simple conditioning model.

One significant government training center, the Federal Executive Institute, has designed its educational methods to fit the adult learning theories of Knowles.[22] Although often viewed as unorthodox by those who experience it the first time, evaluations have demonstrated the program to be highly effective.

CONCLUSION

Human behavior in organizations is an important but complex phenomenon. Rarely is there a simple one-factor explanation. Behavior is characterized by *multiple causalities*. The interaction of personal variables (emotional states, motives, past learnings) and situational variables (group norms, task demands, structures) account for one's performance.

Organizational life has traditionally involved a balancing act between the rational, thinking side of its human members, and the emotional-motivational side. (The term *side* may be an apt word. Current research on physiology and behavior suggests that the left hemisphere of the brain controls the rational, cognitive, objective aspects of our behavior, while the right hemisphere controls the emotional, subjective, intuitive side.) The traditional view of managing people emphasizes exerting control over the nonrational emotional urges of members through strong reliance on structures, rules, and sanctions (rewards and punishments). A contrasting view emphasizes the utilization of the human emotional makeup by providing incentives and situational reinforcements. We will continue to explore these two views from different perspectives in succeeding chapters.

In this chapter we have not dwelt on the unique aspects of public organizations. Basic principles and concepts of human behavior apply across all organizations (at least within Western cultures). The manager, whether in a public or private setting, will do well to understand these basic ideas. Nevertheless, since behavior results from the interaction between the person and the situation, it is also useful to ask, "Are there particular characteristics of public employees' roles which should be accounted for in attempting to understand their motivation, perception, and learning?"

There is a good deal of interesting and informed conjecture about differences between private and public systems, but little solid research. The popular conception furthered by newspaper cartoons and novels is that the typical public employee is not motivated to achieve, not particularly interested in learning, and of relatively narrow perspective. On the positive side, public employees may be seen as loyal and wanting to help others and improve society. If one wished to explore these alleged differences, it would be necessary to ask, "Are these characteristics brought to the job with the employee, or are they due to circumstances within the organization?"

For example, many public organizations have, historically, paid lower wages than comparable private sector firms, and have tried to make up for the difference by providing more attractive fringe benefits that do not so directly affect the legislative budget. These benefits include seniority, longer vacations, cost-of-living increases, and protection against arbitrary firing. These factors may mean that a type of person with certain motivational patterns, such as stronger security and safety needs, is attracted to the agency. But perhaps the motivational equation in an agency is also influenced by internal factors such as managerial style, the fairness of the performance evaluation system, and the availability of promotion opportunities.

In chapter 1 we mentioned some other characteristics of public agencies which may affect employee behavior. These included emphasis on rules and procedures, lack of challenge, atmosphere of criticism and mistrust from outside the agency, few objective performance criteria, and lower status. A manager who wishes to understand the motivation of his or her employees must weigh the above factors and ask, "Do these factors significantly influence either the kinds of employees we attract or the motivational patterns they develop as they work here?"

NOTES TO CHAPTER 3

1. Lewin's work is summarized most usefully by Alfred Marrow in his biography, *The Practical Theorist*, New York: Basic Books, 1969.
2. Elton Mayo, *The Human Problems of an Industrial Civilization*, New York: Macmillan, 1933.

3. A. H. Maslow, *Motivation and Personality*, New York: Harper & Row, 1954.

4. Clayton P. Alderfer, *Existence, Relatedness and Growth: Human Needs in Organizational Settings*, New York: The Free Press, 1972.

5. Frederick Herzberg, *Work and the Nature of Man*, New York: World Publishing Co., 1966, p. 73.

6. David A. Nadler, J. R. Hackman, and E. E. Lawler III, *Managing Organizational Behavior*, Boston: Little, Brown, 1979, Chapter 9.

7. D. A. Nadler and E. E. Lawler III, "Motivation: A Diagnostic Approach," in J. R. Hackman, E. E. Lawler III, and L. W. Porter (eds.), *Perspectives on Behavior in Organizations*, New York: McGraw-Hill, 1977, pp. 26-38.

8. Eric Berne, *Games People Play*, New York: Grove Press, 1964.

9. Albert Ellis and Robert A. Harper, *A Guide to Rational Living*. Hollywood, Calif.: Wilshire, 1973; and *Executive Leadership: A Rational Approach*. Secaucus, N.J.: Citadel, 1972.

10. J. R. P. French and R. P. Caplan, "Organizational Stress and Industrial Strain," in A. Marrow (ed.), *The Failure of Success*, New York: AMACOM, 1972.

11. John D. Adams, "On Consuming Resources: Perspectives on the Management of Stress," in W. Eddy and W. W. Burke (eds.), *Behavioral Science and the Manager's Role*, La Jolla, Calif.: University Associates, 1980.

12. Linda L. Moore and W. B. Eddy, "Manager as Victim: Stress as an Organization Development Issue" in W. Burke and L. Goodstein (eds.), *Trends and Issues in Organization Development: Current Theory and Practice*, San Diego, Calif.: University Associates, 1980, pp. 240-254.

13. Richard W. Wallen, "The Three Types of Executive Personality," *Dun's Review*, February 1963.

14. Sandra Lipsitz Bem, "Psychological Androgyny," in Alice G. Sargent, *Beyond Sex Roles*, St. Paul, Minn.: West Publishing Co., 1977, pp. 319-324.

15. Alice Sargent, "The Androgynous Blend," *Management Review*, October 1978, pp. 60-65.

16. Sheldon S. Zalkind and Timothy W. Costello, "Perception: Implications for Administration," *Administrative Science Quarterly*, vol. 7, 1962, pp. 218-235.

17. B. F. Skinner, *Beyond Freedom and Dignity*, New York: Knopf, 1971. For discussions of behaviorism applied to work see Walter R. Nord, "Beyond the Teaching Machine: The Neglected Area of Operant Conditioning in the Theory and Practice of Management," *Organizational Behavior and Human Performance*, vol. 4, November 1969, pp. 375-401. Also see William F. White, "Skinnerian Theory in Organizations," *Psychology Today*, April, 1972, pp. 34-38+.

18. Alan Tough, *The Adult's Learning Process*, Toronto: Ontario Institute for Studies in Education, 1971.

19. See, for example, Herbert Simon, *The New Sciences of Management Decision*, New York: New York University Press, 1960.

20. Donald A. Schon, *Beyond the Stable State*, New York: Norton, 1971, Chapter 6.

21. Malcolm Knowles, *The Adult Learners: A Neglected Species*, Houston: Gulf, 1973.

22. Paul Buchanan (ed.), *An Approach to Executive Development in Government: The Federal Executive Institute Experience*, Washington, D.C.: National Academy of Public Administration, 1973.

4

Structure and Process in Groups and Organizations

In earlier chapters we discussed organization structure as a primary way of controlling what goes on. In this chapter we will further explore structure as it impacts on the members of the organization, and then move on to look into human interaction *processes*. In order to tie structure and process together in an integrated view of the organization we will take a systems point of view—more specifically that of sociotechnical systems. Finally, we will refer to an issue that has come up before—the problem of the compatibility of human needs and organization demands.

STRUCTURE

Structure can be thought of as the *anatomy* of the organization—those elements that, when put in their proper places, create a mechanism that will function. We most often see the structure depicted in an organization chart such as in Figure 4-1.

Assuming that each of the departments, divisions, and sections has a different task to perform in order for the agency to achieve its overall goal, this chart represents an example of *structural functionalism*. The structure, as represented by the chart, is designed to perform a certain set of functions. In order to make this design operate, it is buttressed with other arrangements. Specialized duties, job assignments, and rules are set up to tell employees how to behave within their functions. Internal control systems are

Structure and Process in Groups and Organizations 73

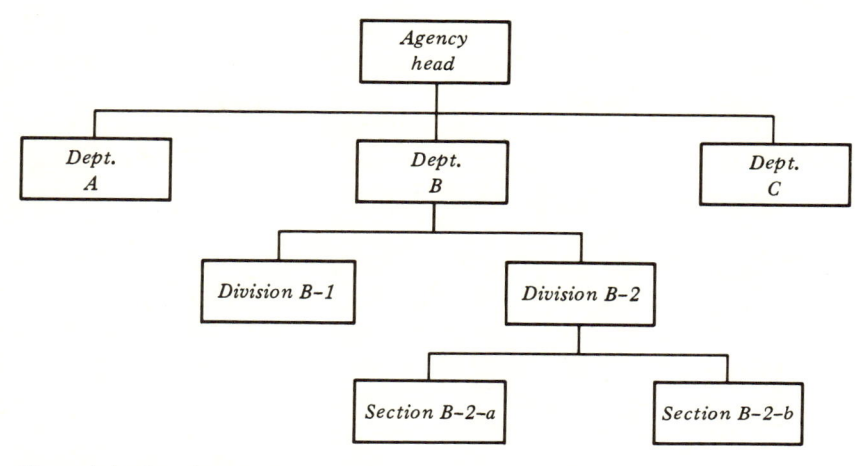

Figure 4-1 Organization Chart

established to monitor and correct the functioning (production and inventory control, accounting, performance appraisal, and so on). Personnel are selected and jobs and machines are engineered to assure the efficient use of human and mechanical energy. In order to exert the necessary control (that is, to make sure people do what they're supposed to) a *hierarchy* is created in which each unit and its personnel are under the control of a higher level of authority. This chain of command from the top to the bottom of the organization also serves as a channel for the flow of information. When the hierarchy is rigidly operated, the only allowable direction of communication flow is vertical (thus the expression, "Going through proper channels").

The hierarchical, structural-functional bureaucracy is the only form of organization that we know of for managing large and complex systems. We may tinker with the structure in various ways in order to improve performance. For example, we may cut out some of the levels to make it flatter in order to speed up response time from the bottom to the top (a more "horizontal" organization). Or we may reorganize by moving the boxes (units) around from one area to another in order to achieve better coordination or control. Or we may assign fewer units or people to a given official in order to allow for more direct supervision (narrowing the span of control). Or we may even institute a participation program in which a more democratic decision-making process takes place. But under all these variations the organization is still a hierarchical bureaucracy.

Innovations such as *matrix organization* and *project teams* are departures from the bureaucratic model and have been used successfully to manage specialized subunits of larger organizations. However, they have not replaced bureaucracy—only augmented it. In these models an individual is assigned from his or her functional department (research, finance, planning, and so on) to an interdisciplinary team of people from several departments. This team works together to complete a project or a major phase of a project. When the activity is finished, the individual goes back to the functional department to be reassigned to another project. The goal of this approach is to provide greater flexibility to bring human resources to bear on problems. It was developed in the aerospace industry as a way of moving several complex projects through a technical organization without the usual rigidities and delays.[1] Figure 4-2 shows one way of illustrating a matrix.

For several reasons governmental organizations are particularly susceptible to having their structures criticized, second guessed, and revised. For one thing, the structure and those who inhabit the higher levels of the hierarchy are clearly visible. Reporters and politicians, whose understanding of the intricacies of the complex organizations may be superficial, can readily find a scapegoat in the structure. Too few people are assigned to a given problem area, it may appear, or too many, or the rules and procedures have not been updated to fit new circumstances. Or there are too many units under one executive, and some are not being given proper attention. In addition, the problem may be made more difficult by political decision makers who mandate the structures but don't have to run them.

The agencies of the federal government are in a near-perpetual state of being reorganized. Presidential commissions such as the Hoover Commissions, congressional committees, the Office of Management and the Budget, the General Accounting Office, and various nongovernmental research or consulting organizations all try their hand at rearranging the structure. State and local governments and other agencies often experience the same efforts, for example, reorganizing a group of local jurisdictions into a consoli-

	Project 1	*Project Authority* Project 2	Project 3
Functional Units	Project Manager	Project Manager	Project Manager
Unit A (research)			
Unit B (finance)			
Unit C (legal)			
Unit D (planning)			
	Project Team #1	Project Team #2	Project Team #3

Line or Staff Authority

Figure 4-2 A Matrix Organization Structure

dated metrogovernment. If the problems of the agency are truly structural, the reorganization may be beneficial. If the problems stem from other factors, the structural changes are likely to be purely cosmetic or even damaging. And therein lies the need to look at the process.

The dilemma with structure is that it can only *organize, enable,* and *influence*. It cannot control in an absolute sense, and it cannot assure that desired outcomes happen. In fact, unanticipated and unwanted consequences are highly probable, because much of what goes on in organizations has to do with the dynamics of human interaction and therefore cannot be wholly predetermined by structures. Behavior, as we have said, derives from the interaction between situational factors—including the organizational structure—and the characteristics of the person.

SOCIOTECHNICAL SYSTEMS

In searching for a term and a concept that would clearly describe the interaction and interdependence among humans and with the other aspects of the organization, behavioral scientists at Britain's

Tavistock Institute coined the term *sociotechnical system*.[2] The term denotes the important notion that there is only one overall system, with the human interactions and technical-mechanical aspects as components. You cannot separate the "human element" from the rest—no matter how hard you try. This is why structural reorganizations, new computers, and redesigned work methods do not necessarily make for higher productivity. It is also why, under a different set of circumstances, those three measures could lead to considerably higher productivity.

Those who have advanced the concept of sociotechnical systems have done so for reasons other than theoretical elegance. The sociotechnical view provides a way of thinking about programs of change, or *interventions,* which take into account and capitalize on the system characteristics. According to Pasmore and Sherwood

Socio-technical system interventions are organization development techniques that typically involve the restructuring of work methods, rearrangements of technology or the redesign of organizational social structures. The objective is to optimize the relationship between the social or human systems of the organization and the technology used by the organization to product output.[3]

The application of sociotechnical strategies can, when fully developed, follow a rigorous rational-logical process, but one that takes into account the human variables (motives, values, perceptions, and so on) as well as the mechanical ones.

Examples of government agencies that have a particularly significant mix of social and technical components include military units with sophisticated weapons systems, health care organizations, and highly computerized agencies like most vehicle license bureaus. Even in labor-intensive units such as public schools, however, the sociotechnical model is still applicable.

Another concept used by systems theorists, and one of particular importance in public agencies, is the distinction between *closed systems* and *open systems.* A closed system is a self-contained unit with solid, impermeable borders or boundaries and no interaction with other systems. Although organizations as completely closed systems probably do not exist, an example of a relatively closed system would be a commune that raises most of its own food and fiber, educates its children, keeps to itself, and attempts to keep the rest of society from influencing it. Another might be a university that does things pretty much the same way year after year, is not much influenced by students, parents, or politicians, spends a lot of energy on its own internal affairs, and has an elaborate set of traditions and values (such as academic freedom) to protect its boundaries from incursions by external forces. Many governmental agencies are, of course, perceived by citizens as closed, in that they are hard to get into and hard to influence.

An open system, on the other hand, is characterized by permeable boundaries and ongoing transactions and communications with other systems. There are many parts of the system that regularly interact with outside parties, and a good measure of what the organization achieves is affected by its *interdependence* with other systems. Relatively open systems include those municipal governments that collaborate with other governments, have provisions for a variety of kinds of citizen participation, are affected by a multitude of federal regulatory and funding agencies, and are controlled by a vigorous and changing political process.

Traditional models of organization were based largely on closed system notions. The organization, whether an army, a church, or a factory, was assumed to set its own course and manage its own affairs with minimal interaction with other systems. There were few provisions for transactions with the outside world except at the very top of the organization—the board of directors or owners—who dealt with government officials and other important persons. This tradition has been one of the factors that has led agencies to be perceived as unresponsive and uncooperative. If the underlying assumption is that the internal business of the organization is the important aspect, and this assumption is supported by professionalism and technology, there is little likelihood that much energy will be diverted to interactions with the environment.

Managing an open system and taking into account the sociotechnical realities is, in many ways, a more difficult and demanding task than managing a traditional semiclosed, mechanistic system. The term *management by exception* has, for example, been used to denote the philosophy that the manager sets the mechanism into motion and then has only to watch for and deal with the variations, rule infractions, and breakdowns. The manager of the

78 Public Organization Behavior and Development

open sociotechnical system, however, needs a different conception of his or her role—a role more akin to a social systems engineer who continually monitors, adjusts, and redesigns the internal processes and manages their interactions (or "interfaces") with other systems. There is only so much energy available in any system (human time, strength, skills, and resources). This energy may be used toward productive and rewarding activities or drained away or wasted on internal or external concerns that bear no payoff. One way of conceptualizing the system and identifying its major components is contained in Weisbord's model shown in Figure 4-3.

A MODEL OF ORGANIZATION

Anyone who studies organizations must make decisions about what to emphasize and what frame of reference to use. These decisions are made on the basis of all things that influence human choices—interests, values, experiences, positions, and so on. Managers, for example, focus on different issues than do researchers. As we have said, earlier approaches to the study of organizations focused on structure and rules and authority patterns. That is, they looked at the organization chart, the chain of command, procedures and rewards/punishments. Managers often talk about organizations as being made up of *men, money, materials,* and *machinery.* A newer, and for our purposes more useful, scheme for viewing what goes on in an organization was developed by Weisbord (see Figure 4-3). It emphasizes the human interaction aspects and the role of the leader as elements of the sociotechnical system.

The six boxes in Figure 4-3 represent six organizational processes which, taken together, determine how an organization will function. (In real life the processes are, or course, not as separated as they are in the drawing.) The top box, entitled *Purposes,* represents activities that in public agencies include legislation, policymaking, goal setting, and clarification of the mission. It used to be said that these activities belong outside the agency, that the administrator should leave policymaking to elected officials. This view was not realistic because administrators, with their technical expertise, firsthand view of the problems, and high personal invest-

Structure and Process in Groups and Organizations 79

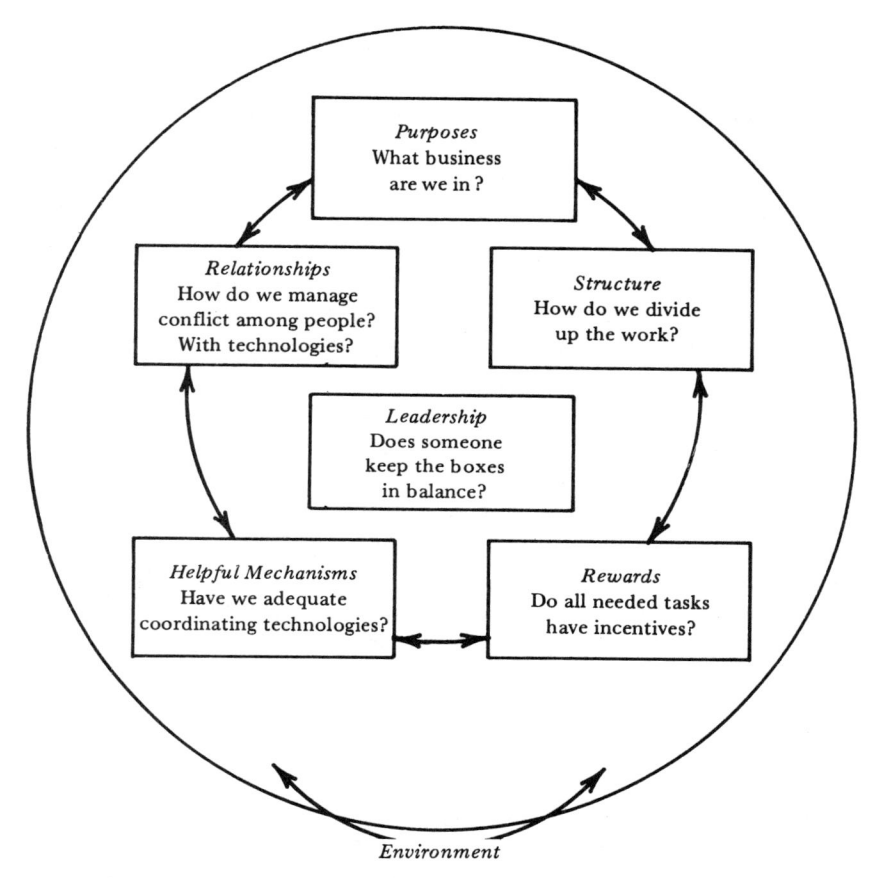

Figure 4-3 Six-Box Model of Organizational Diagnosis (Source: M. Weisbord, "Organizational diagnosis: Six places to look for trouble with or without a theory," *Group and Organization Studies,* vol. 1, 1976, p. 430. Reproduced with permission of M. Weisbord and Organization Research and Development, a division of Block Petrella Associates.)

ment, *do* get involved in policymaking in a variety of ways. They identify problems that need attention, suggest policies, draft legislation, provide information, and sometimes lobby informally or formally. From the point of view of the human element this involvement in policy is highly desirable, because the level of the organization's commitment to goals that members have no part in setting or influencing is apt to be low. Furthermore, involvement in discussing purposes is necessary in order to be sure goals are clearly stated, understood, and agreed to.

The second box in clockwise progression is *Structure,* how work is divided up and organized. In many ways structure is the most visible aspect of the organization's dynamics. Almost everyone is used to looking at the organization chart, tracing the lines of authority and information flow, and second-guessing about the most efficient way of allocating duties to specialized subunits. There are, of course, many human implications to structural arrangements. Questions of who does what work and how they feel about it, determining competence and evaluating performance, formal and informal communication processes, and arranging the flow of work from one unit to another are examples of human factors that interact with structural factors.

The next box is named *Rewards.* People are willing to work in organizations because in so doing they can exchange their efforts for rewards or incentives that have value to them. A major preoccupation of applied behavioral science has been the study of human motivation. What needs do employees have that affect their work? What incentives and working conditions bring about increases in productivity? What factors cause low morale, lack of commitment, and dissatisfaction?

By now it should be understood that no manager can motivate an employee. Motivation is an internal process. All we can do is attempt to arrange aspects of the situation (pay, working conditions, task design, supervisory styles, and so on) in such a way that they have a positive effect on productivity and satisfaction. The manager's job is to acquire both the resources and the insights necessary to provide a good reward system. It is also important to eliminate as many as possible of the disincentives or negative rewards.

Helpful Mechanisms have to do with coordinating the activities of people and groups so that the various efforts mesh smoothly and multiply productivity. Even though structures and incentives are properly set up, poor coordination means subunits working at cross purposes, wasted motion, and lack of adequate information. Procedures, information systems, meetings, and budgets can, if well implemented, be helpful mechanisms. They can also be nonhelpful or even obstructive. Red tape, ineffective meetings, and arbitrary and outdated rules are examples of helpful mechanisms gone wrong.

When humans in an organization become overly controlled by

mechanisms that are no longer helpful, when these mechanisms are not changed even though they are weighing down the organization, and/or when people hide behind the mechanisms rather than solving problems, the public labels the agency *bureaucratic.*

The last box on the perimeter of Weisbord's model is *Relationships.* Interactions among members are human interactions, even though many of the mechanisms are structural and procedural. In organizations in which there is high interdependence (people must rely closely upon each other) the quality of these interactions exerts a strong impact on the organization's ability to do its work. For example, members of an urban police force often work in highly interdependent situations, as do members of a commission or board dealing with a sensitive problem. If there is conflict, competition, and misunderstanding, and if these processes are not well managed, the interfaces in the organization are likely to be troublesome. Another important relationship in organizations is that between people and technology.

The final box in the model, the one in the center, is *Leadership.* It is the leader's job to monitor the other six aspects to make sure they are in balance and functioning properly. This view is consonant with Likert's concept of the "linking pin" function. An important aspect of the leadership role is to link together through communication the many groups, units, and functions in an organization. The leader, who often has membership in a number of different subgroups, thus has an opportunity to help build cooperation and resolve conflicts.[4] Weisbord points out that too frequently in public organizations, the leader attempts to smooth over conflicts and anxieties at the expense of achieving goals.

Two more things about the six-box model should be mentioned. One is that there are both *formal* and *informal* aspects to the activities described in each box. That is, some things about policies, for example, are formal. They are written down according to prescribed rules, procedures, and laws, officially endorsed by the authorities, and cannot be changed except in certain preset ways. Other aspects of the policy process are informal, including how policies are perceived and interpreted, how people feel about them, and if and how they are applied in actual practice. There are similar formal and informal aspects to the other areas as well. A common example of the importance of informal activity has to do with the helpful mechanisms, where a good deal of on-the-spot adaptation and problem solving is often required to keep the rules and regulations from bringing the organization to a halt.

The final point about the model is that the organization functions in constant interaction with its environment. Not only is there input at the level of policy, but outside groups get involved in the other activities. Customers or constituents influence structure when they claim that the agency is not organized appropriately to deliver services to them. Labor unions and professional associations influence reward systems. Rules and procedures are influenced by regulatory bodies such as the Occupational Health and Safety Administration (OSHA). No public organization operates in isolation, and no agency can, in this day and age, limit environmental input to top policymaking or legislative levels.

Weisbord's model is useful in providing an overview of the areas of the organization's functioning that involve the major focus of this book—the people. The people and technologies taken together depict a *sociotechnical system*—an interacting and interrelated series of components that form the total organization.

HUMAN INTERACTION PROCESSES

In this section we will further explore the social process aspects of systems (the technical subsystems are outside the scope of this book). A key point is that traditional structural theories had very little to say about social interaction processes, except to presume to control them with rules and regulations. There are many ways to think about social interaction variables. The following discussion provides one relatively straightforward way of viewing human social behavior within and among groups.[6]

Communication

Organizations as systems operate on the basis of the exchange of information among levels, units, and individuals. In a real sense, communication is the nerve network of the organization. When the flow from those who have the data to those who need it is

Structure and Process in Groups and Organizations 83

rapid, complete, accurate, and properly channeled, one major area important to the organization's performance is contributing effectively. If, on the other hand, the flow of information necessary for decision making is slow, incomplete, inaccurate, and tangled up in the structure, errors and animosities are likely to occur. And, as experienced managers know, attempting to order or mandate that good communication will occur is of dubious value. One must find ways to understand the communication process and work internally toward its improvement.

There are any number of reasons why organization communications break down. Practically every management text has a chapter or two on communications. One can speak of communication *networks* (the formal and informal pathways through which messages flow); *barriers* to communication (places in the network that stop the flow); *interference* from other messages; problems with the *sender* (lack of clarity, unwillingness to be open); problems with the *receiver* (insensitivity, defensiveness, lack of concern); and simply the amount of emphasis the organization places on effective communication.

A sociotechnical system view of the manager's role in relation to organizational communication is that structuring communication by establishing guidelines, specifying proper formal channels, and generating reports and forms are possibly useful but often insufficient. Although some aspects of the communication process can be routinized and made highly reliable (such as electronic information storage and retrieval subsystems), the human elements cannot be successfully dealt with in that fashion. As we have noted before, while people are in some ways information processors, their rational handling of data is interfered with by their emotions, motives, perception, and past learnings. Thus, when attempting to understand and improve overall organizational communications, the social process is important.

We will look briefly at two separate but related aspects of the organizational communication process—interpersonal communication and organizational communication networks.

Interpersonal communication, the exchange of information and meanings between two or more individuals in a meeting, interview, or other setting, must be looked at as an aspect of a human relationship. The first thing to remember is that the vast majority (some say all) of interpersonal communications involves an attempt to *influence,* not merely to inform. As initiator of the communication, we want the other person (the receiver) to do something we want done, or to see things our way, or to view us or treat us in a certain way. Thus, we often communicate at several levels. We provide information, we appeal to emotions, we offer rewards (either directly or subtly), we threaten (again, directly or subtly), we withhold some of the information and stress other parts of it, we build ourselves up as good and wise authorities, we dispute the other person's views or values.

If we are on the receiving end of the communication, we have to cope with being influenced and, at the same time, we are likely to attempt to, in turn, influence the other party. We evaluate what we hear as we listen for the hidden as well as the obvious meanings. We filter out that which is distasteful, we put up our defenses in order to keep from being coerced, and we may play-act in order to get across the picture of ourselves that we feel will be most advantageous.

The point of this description is to demonstrate the many levels at which communication between people can become blocked and distorted. Courses on how to speak clearly or on writing succinct memos are unlikely to go very far in assuring a vigorous and viable organizational communication process.

People who are highly effective interpersonal communicators have the capacity to tune in at several levels simultaneously so as to understand fully the *meanings* the other person is attempting to convey (sometimes called "sensitivity"). They are also able to understand and control their own emotional responses so that these do not act as barriers in receiving and sending accurate information. There are no magic keys to the acquisition of such skills. Self-understanding, practice under conditions in which feedback is possible, and strong concern for what others think and feel are useful techniques.

When one moves from a discussion of interpersonal communication to the broader concern of how the necessary information gets transmitted throughout the system, the variables change somewhat. The traditional model of organization is best at moving information from the top down, under the assumption that the best perspective and intelligence exist at the senior management levels and the need is to get the information transmitted down to those at lower levels so that they will know what to do. This approach does less well in relaying information from the bottom up, sideways from one unit to another, or diagonally from a lower level unit in one division to a higher level unit in another division. The problem in the modern sociotechnical system is that one-way communication is not adequate. Problems or conflicts may go undetected until damage has been done; the ability to check whether directives are received and understood may be inadequate; the need to pool information from multiple sources at different levels to solve problems may not be met; and attempts to develop cooperation among different parts of the system may fail because of slow and restricted communication. In later chapters when we will describe techniques of organization design and change, we will have more to say about building effective communication systems.

In addition to internal communication processes there are also important needs to communicate to groups outside the agency. The factors we have been discussing also apply to communications with citizens, clients, contractors, and legislators.

Before leaving this topic it is important to point out that what are commonly referred to as communication problems may be symptoms of other organizational difficulties. For example, two individuals who are in conflict are often said to have communication problems, a statement which presumes that a fuller sharing of information and viewpoints would correct the situation. This might be true, but it might also be the case that the conflict is due to other factors such as intense rivalry, divergent interests, or basic value differences that additional information would not resolve. I was recently asked to consult with a community agency in which the individual in charge was described by other key personnel as having a communication problem with the rest of the organization. After a good deal of investigation it turned out that the manager was communicating what *he thought* other members should know and doing so reasonably effectively. The problem was a mix-up in expectations. Members were not receiving the *kind* of information they wanted and felt they needed. Instead of working to obtain different kinds of information they were simply chalking their frustrations up to "poor communications."

Cooperation

Chester Barnard, one of the first practicing managers to gain eminence as a theorist, viewed the need to build cooperation among organizational subunits as the crucial function of the executive.[7] The pooling and meshing of the efforts of many people is the reason for establishing organizations. As we have seen, the traditional organizational model established specialized functional units and sought to coordinate their efforts through a hierarchy and a set of control systems. Although there is danger of getting caught in semantic games, it is useful to distinguish between coordination and cooperation. Coordination connotes a meshing of efforts because of externally imposed controls and sanctions. Cooperation implies a more willing, internally motivated process. The significant difference is that the manager can order coordination, but he or she cannot order cooperation. Cooperation, working together because of a desire and willingness to do so, and/or out of a belief that there will be mutual benefit, is a human interaction process.

The problem of fostering cooperation is one of the prime challenges to managers in sociotechnical systems. The high degrees of interdependence among subsystems means that each unit must be aware of and responsive to not only its own needs and realities, but also those of sister units. Such responsible and responsive behavior must become a part of the value system of the organization. Die-hard competition among individuals and units is often destructive, in spite of the fact that society emphasizes competition in other endeavors, such as athletics.

Cooperation is sometimes difficult to achieve in public systems because of the variety of overall organizational goals and also because of divided political allegiances. Many governmental organizations do not have a single overall goal (such as manufacturing and selling a can opener), but, rather, pursue many separate goals. For example, subunits within a city government conduct such varied activities as collecting trash, providing water, inspecting buildings, fighting fires, and hosting conventions. While it is easy for the city administrator to see the many ways in which subunits can usefully cooperate, the view from the inside is different as units jockey for budget dollars, recognition, personnel, and influence. The problem is complicated by the fact that many of the units have political constituencies that press them to move in directions not necessarily cooperative with other units. As an illustration, neighborhood groups may demand much more rigorous inspections of remodeled and refurbished houses in order to protect neighborhood property values. Such a move may cause more work for the legal department, complaints to city council members, tax complications for the revenue department, and allegations to the human relations commission if there are possible racial or ethnic overtones. All these complications are likely to stress the spirit of cooperation among units.

There are several approaches to increasing interunit cooperation. The manager sets an example by the kind of cooperative behavior he or she exhibits, such as, "Let's don't move ahead any farther on this project until we check it out with Unit D. It may have implications for them that we haven't thought of. Also there may be ways they can help us." Contrast this with "Don't say anything to Unit D about this project yet. We don't want them trying to move in on us until we get it nailed down."

Another avenue to collaboration utilizes sociotechnical systems design strategies. Such strategies frequently involve planning projects in which members of various subunits participate together in setting up cooperative processes, communication paths, and work practices. We will describe these techniques in greater detail in Chapter 7.

Yet another strategy, often related to system design, utilizes behavioral science group and intergroup training techniques. This field of organization development teaches organization members skills for more effective collaboration. We will also discuss it in more detail later.

A final point on cooperation. Although from the point of view of internal system functioning it is clearly advantageous, one does not find agreement that cooperation should replace competition in all cases. One view is that employees are spurred on to higher achievement by competition. This view doubtless has merit in a situation in which, for example, salespersons sell on commission in different territories and thus are not interdependent. Such a philosophy, however, bears close scrutiny if one is dealing with the various subsections of a municipal budget department, with each subsection vying for a bigger share of the pie for its constituent departments. Another reservation about building cooperative relations applies particularly to government agencies. The concept of *checks and balances* denotes an arrangement in which various units are explicitly charged with not establishing cooperative systems, but, rather, checking up on each other to see that there are no wrongdoings. In fact, the term *collusion* refers to cooperative arrangements that serve improper purposes. Thus, before endorsing the need for cooperation in *all* circumstances, it is necessary to evaluate the possibility of negative consequences.

Control

We have noted before that control is a goal and a function of the formal structure. It involves hierarchy, rules, sanctions, and work procedures. The other aspect of control is that it is an interpersonal process. It involves individuals' needs and wishes for power to exert influence over others. It also involves people's feelings about being controlled—the degree and the condition under which they accept or resist influence from other people.

Management, of course, involves the influencing of others' behaviors in various ways, some through what is sometimes referred to as *official* power (rules, position, rewards, and punishments) and some through *personal power* (developing respect and rapport with others so that they feel positive about obeying and cooperating). In most modern organizations managers do not have anything approaching absolute control, although some inexperienced managers may mistakenly think they have. The challenge is to exert enough *influence* (partial control) to assure that the required tasks are performed without eliciting unnecessary resistance.

There is a good deal of variation in the degree to which individuals desire to exert control over others. Some of us have very low control needs—we are content to let others pursue their own pathways and to allow events to play themselves out as they will. Others have high needs for control. They want to be in charge, to organize things, to act strongly to see that their wishes are carried out. Individuals with high needs for control are likely to seek careers such as management, law enforcement, or budgeting, which allow them to exercise these needs.

William Schutz developed a psychological inventory that measures the need to express control in one's behavior.[9] The inventory, the Fundamental Interpersonal Relations Orientation (FIRO), also measures the other side of the coin—the degree to which people want to be controlled. Those high on *wanted control* prefer to be told what to do, to be led, to play a subordinate role. Those with low scores on wanted control are the opposite. They rebel at too much pressure for conformity and try to avoid being put in situations where they lose self-control.

These varying individual differences in expressed and wanted control, combined with the controls built into the hierarchical structure, are bound to cause problems upon occasion. Many of the strategies devised by managers are at least in part attempts to resolve control issues. Management by objectives (originally referred to by McGregor as "management by integration and self-control") gains control by mutual agreement on goals.[10] Participative management programs assume employees will be motivated to act responsively (control themselves) if allowed to make some of the decisions. Job enrichment-enlargement projects assume that employees will be more satisfied and productive if they are given control over a larger and more varied sphere of work.

Control issues in organizations are never fully resolved. People have varying and conflicting control needs. No decision-making strategy is likely to resolve all conflicts under all circumstances. The manager needs to understand clearly his or her own needs for giving and receiving control, as well as those of superiors and subordinates. The fact that managers in public organizations are usually held strictly accountable for the behavior of their subordinate civil servants increases the tendency to exert control. The delicate balance—just enough, but not too much, control—is an elusive goal.

Conflict

Conflict is an integral part of human interactions, and thus a part of the daily life of organizations. It arises from a number of sources and usually cannot be legislated away by the formal organization. It may be controlled for a while, but often breaks out again if not resolved. Some conflicts arise because individuals or groups engage in win-lose competitive activities in which someone will lose and their needs will be frustrated. The *frustration-aggression hypothesis,* an old principle in psychology, asserts that aggressive behavior results when a person's attempts to reach a goal are blocked. Aggression leads to conflict as others are attacked for one's problems and failures. Other conflicts result from strong value differences, personal dislikes, and hostile behavior by one or more parties.

In many ways a complex organization is rigged for conflict. As separate work units develop their own in-group loyalties and cohesiveness, they tend to devalue other groups unless cross-group understandings are carefully built. In order to reach organizational goals top management hands different subgoals to its units. These goals may seem incompatible to members, and in some cases they may be. Furthermore, the size and complexity of many organizations set up "we-they" contrasts: management-union, blue collar–white collar, professional-nonprofessional, line-staff, central office–field office, and so on. Each of these distinctions holds within it the potential for separate goals, misunderstanding, competition, poor communication, blaming, and conflict.

Conflict may occur at several levels—intrapersonal (within an individual), interpersonal, intergroup, and intraorganizational. Intrapersonal conflicts, such as inability to make a decision, violation of one's own values (for example, by cheating), or by having to do a distasteful thing (like firing someone), are usually manifested by stress and anxiety and may or may not spill out into the organization. Interpersonal and intergroup conflicts, on the other hand, are organizational phenomena.

As we suggested earlier, most organizations are not well equipped to deal with conflict. The first tendency is usually to ignore it, sweep it under the rug, pretend it doesn't exist. If the conflict is minor and temporary, such an approach may work. If it is basic and severe, it will not die out spontaneously if avoided.

In spite of many research efforts, the social sciences still cannot provide sure-fire methods for resolving conflict.[11] In addition, some of the suggestions are counterintuitive (disagree with our basic assumptions) because we have built-in biases about conflict. For example, the first reactions of many people to a conflict situation are to admonish the warring parties to stop ("fighting won't solve anything") or to provide rational arguments aimed at resolving the issue. If we stop to think, most of us realize such efforts are unlikely to work for long because they do not deal with causes. More successful are conflict management techniques that involve steps such as (1) acknowledging and owning up to the conflict, (2) suspending blaming the other party and, instead, expressing one's own feelings and perceptions, (3) opening up communication and sharing cross perceptions (how each group views the other), (4) establishing joint problem-solving processes, and (5) having the parties sit down with a third-party consultant or mediator to work out a resolution.

Approaches to dealing with conflict in the traditional organization are usually quite different. They tend to rely on rules and structures and involve such measures as isolating the parties to the conflict from each other so that they do not have to interact, imposing a resolution from an authority above the parties in the hierarchy, redesigning position descriptions and procedures to clarify inconsistencies and overlaps, or ordering the fighters to cease their "emotional and irrational behavior." Compulsory and binding arbitration in labor disputes is a common example of an imposed solution to an unsolved conflict.

Commitment

In the ideal organization, the employees are highly *committed*. They express belief in and adherence to the organization's goals and methods. Committed employees are self-motivated in the sense that they meet some of their own needs while striving toward organizational goals. Such a state of affairs is highly desirable because it minimizes the wasted time and energy spent checking up on people and enforcing rules with sanctions. It also calls forth the best of employees' potential and minimizes waste.

High levels of commitment are not easy to achieve and are even harder to maintain. When an organization or subunit is new and when those who work there have participated in building it, commitment is usually high. Goals are clear, people's beliefs in the goals are high, and there is pride in achievement. As organizations grow older, larger, and more bureaucratic identification with goals and purposes is often replaced by enforced adherence to rules and procedures. Under such conditions members may commit themselves not to the employing organization but to other systems—unions, informal cliques, specialized subunits (such as the accounting department), or a profession ("I am first and foremost committed to being a professional engineer").

Increasing commitment in large, mature organizations is not an easy task. Human relations ventures such as "Why I like my agency" contests, recognition dinners, and house organs (agency newsletters) are apt to have minimal and temporary impact. In the last two chapters on effectiveness and change we will discuss organizational improvement strategies that contain commitment-building elements.

Cohesiveness

Cohesiveness is a concept not entirely separate from commitment, but it connotes a strong identification with the group or organization, feelings of support from the relationships, and a desire to stay with the group and keep it together.

Cohesiveness is a two-edged sword. Research indicates that highly effective work groups and teams are characterized by cohesiveness. Units that take pride in themselves, provide support to their members, and work to establish a pleasant atmosphere are obviously desirable. On the other hand, the manager must beware of units that become so cohesive that they grow insulated away from the rest of the system and place their own goals and values above those of the organization.

Because of the social relatedness needs we discussed earlier, many human beings have a propensity to move into group situations and to strive to build lasting, cohesive relationships. This natural tendency exerts powerful forces on any organization. Some units will manifest cohesiveness through strong team spirit and pride in accomplishment. Others will manifest their cohesiveness through hostility or competitiveness toward another group. Overall organizational cohesiveness operates the same way. Its positive sides are pride, low turnover, mutual assistance on problems, and a supportive atmosphere. Negative aspects are a self-protectiveness that conceals errors, an inward focus that overlooks new developments and needs on the outside, and a tendency to underrate other organizations. Organizations that are subject to outside pressure or suspicion, such as law enforcement agencies and inspectors, are likely to develop high levels of cohesiveness and isolation.

Trust

Trust is one of the most important but intangible of all interpersonal process variables. It has been studied extensively, yet a useful definition is difficult to find. The central issue is *risk*. To what extent can people be themselves—say what's on their minds, try out tentative ideas, forget about projecting a correct image, express anger? Or to what extent do they have to protect themselves by not risking, being closed, and saying what they think others want to hear as opposed to what is really on their mind. Trust makes for healthier human systems—better communication, more truth, less energy spent on games and cover-up.[12] Organizations with low trust levels create yes-men and other conformists who, because they operate at the safety-security need levels, contribute almost nothing to moving the organization on to new achievements.

As we suggested earlier in a different context, public organizations are particularly susceptible to loss of trust. Many forces within and outside, including political interests, media, and pressure groups, make it risky to behave authentically. When saying what is on one's mind may lead to being quoted in public, perhaps out of context or perhaps having the statement used against you, the trust level is almost certain to be lowered.

As is true for the other process issues, strategies for raising trust are not typically found in the traditional organizational manual. Structural arrangement or rules are not of much help. Developing trust requires clear statements on the part of top management regarding the values that the organization seeks to achieve. No retribution for speaking the truth, encouragement of risk taking, no sacred cows, team development sessions involving frank communication across levels, and evaluation based on long-term goal achievement rather than image are some of the typical ingredients. These are usually followed by a long period of testing in which employees take small risks and than wait to see the effects before deciding to trust.[13]

Intimacy

Organizational behavior, as we have seen, involves more than formal, impersonal, businesslike interactions. Weber's notion of "formalistic impersonality" notwithstanding, feelings creep into human transactions. Several facets of this reality need to be considered in relation to the operation of the sociotechnical system.

Individuals as well as organizations differ in regard to their styles and desires for close personal relations. Some are cool, formal, and distant, while others demonstrate warmth, informality, and a tendency to reach out to include others. When such characteristics vary within an organization or one of its subunits, some people may feel ignored or unsupported while others feel threatened by being approached too closely. These variations in feelings about inclusion and intimacy are significant in several settings. Some people enjoy meetings; others find them distasteful. Some find involvement of several people in joint decisionmaking and planning to be natural and productive; others find it troublesome and a waste of time. Some people make many friends and socialize outside the office. Others prefer to be alone. All these various styles need to be taken into account when considering managerial programs and policies.

Another facet of the impact of human intimacy on organizations is sexual relations—a topic that is frequently discussed but studied very little. Many texts never mention this factor, but when one talks to members about what is *really* going on in the organization's internal political life, sex is frequently a part of the picture. There is no question about the fact that sex represents a powerful human motive and it should not be surprising that it emerges sometimes in organizational settings. In addition to the development of a relationship between two people for the purpose of sexual gratification and intimacy, sex is also *used* for manipulation, bribery, and blackmail. Although the occasional newspaper exposé of "sex running rampant" in some agency obviously depicts an extreme case, it is the naive manager who does not keep an eye out for the side effects of human attraction and sexuality.

CLIMATE

All these processes: communication, cooperation, control, conflict, commitment, cohesiveness, trust, and intimacy, as well as others we haven't discussed, interact to form the social aspects of the

Commitment	Cohesiveness	Trust	Intimacy
Communication	Cooperation	Control	Conflict

Figure 4-4 The Work Climate. Human interaction processes in organizations

sociotechnical system. A common term for the overall impact of all of these is *climate*. Some prefer the term *work culture*. It heavily influences how the people respond to the requirements of the system—in Weisbord's terms, to the purposes, structure, rewards, mechanisms, relationships, and leadership. Figure 4-4 shows the eight process variables. It also indicates that in most situations the achievement of commitment, cohesiveness, trust, and intimacy depends upon the quality of communication, cooperation, control, and conflict resolutions.

INFLUENCES ON PROCESS

A little thought will make it clear that the processes we have discussed do not exist in pure, uncontaminated form. A number of forces both within and outside the organization act to complicate and confuse the processes.

Professionalism

Public agencies are significantly affected by professional employees and their professional values. Engineers, accountants, lawyers, nurses, and others bring with them into the organization not only skills, but also a set of values, instilled in professional schools, publications, and conventions, about appropriate ways of functioning. These values affect the organizational processes—the way people work together—sometimes in useful ways, sometimes not. Many professionals split their allegiances between the organization and their profession, thus affecting their level of commitment ("I'd much rather leave the agency than give up being an engineer"). Others find it difficult to engage in collaborative activities, including spending time in meetings, because of their emphasis on expertise and individualized efforts. Still others find the development of human interaction skills necessary for managerial success to be a waste of their time. The study of professionalism is a well-developed subfield in social science, and even a cursory summary would use up more space than we have available. Perhaps a useful final generalization is that professionals who participate in organizations as employees carry with them an extra set of identifications that are reinforced by others of the same subgroup and require additional understanding.

Biases and Stereotypes

It is well known in life as well as in science that we tend to have problems with those who are different from us. When the differences are at the individual level, when we have trouble with a colleague who doesn't do his share, for example, we think of it as a personality conflict. When we have a reaction to an entire group of people (women, minorities, politicians, Feds, and so on) and attribute certain characteristics to all of them, the term is *prejudice*. Differences and people's emotional responses to them affect the process of organizations: "Those accountants in the budget department can't understand *our* problems—why talk to them?" The women in the social service unit aren't doing what they're supposed to, "but we can't confront them about it because they're women." The black administrator "has a problem" because he can't get the whites in his unit to trust him. When injected into people's otherwise complex interactions, all these stereotypes further contribute to difficulties in getting people to work together successfully.

Politics

So-called office politics, the internal informal forming of allegiances, jockeying for power, and trading off information and advantages, goes on in all organizations. It affects the process in many obvious ways—competition and control struggles replace cooperation, trust is lowered because of the need for self-protection, and the goals of the unit are replaced, in part, by personal power or security moves.

The other kind of politics, external partisan activities, also exerts significant impact on the process. We have discussed several of these in other contexts. They include blocked communication and lowering of trust levels out of fear of exposure and punishment, high needs to appear to be in control, and instability due to a changing political system. The pressures of the political system are so severe that they have led to many efforts to insulate the organization, including the civil service merit systems, the Hatch Act, which prohibits partisan political activity by public employees, and various laws regulating business transactions such as purchasing.

Complexity

One of the aspects of public management which affects its functionings in many ways is the vast complexity of the governmental system. "Big government" has become permanent in most developed countries. In the United States the political, executive, legislative, and judicial systems interact, often in adversary relationships, from the very top to the very bottom of the Federal government. These systems also have an impact on state and local governments. A government manager operates in an ever-changing matrix of forces and demands from constituents, courts, regulatory commisions, budgeteers, and the central office. Conditions are similar in other countries. Figuring out how to understand and maneuver within the complex system often becomes a preoccupation.

Under such conditions the traditional conceptions of the well-organized and efficient manager break down. Instead of presiding over rationally functioning administrative processes, the manager is likely to spend significant energy trying to make sense out of ambiguity. These realities led public administrator and educator Harlan Cleveland to observe that the successful future executive will need to understand how to operate under conditions of "polyguity" (more complex even than ambiguity).[14]

Changing Work Values

If there ever was a time when the average worker felt totally positive about doing tasks designed by someone else, taking orders, and following the notebook full of rules and procedures, that time is past. It is becoming popular to say that workers are dissatisfied, alienated, and turned off and although there is a question of proportions, the generalization is no doubt true. Many workers want to be told why. They demand that authority be based on competency rather than tenure and that humanitarian concerns be considered along with output goals. They are concerned about the quality of their work lives. It does the senior manager little good to bemoan the fact that college graduates aren't like they used to be. All these factors need to be taken into account in a strategy to deal with the process issues of an organization.

GROUPS IN ORGANIZATIONS

Implicit in the view of organizations as sociotechnical systems is the fact that a system is comprised of interacting and interdependent subsystems—groups. Or, put another way, an organization is built up of a collection of groups, each with a different purpose or function and each with its own unique characteristics. In this sense, an organization is a "group of groups," or, perhaps more appropriately in public systems, a coalition of groups. Thus one can look at organizational functioning as it occurs within groups and as it occurs among groups. The structural factors we discussed earlier and the process issues explored in the next section apply to both levels—*intragroup* and *intergroup*. The traditional approach has been to attempt to control and regularize behavior within and among groups through rules and procedures. As we saw earlier, the Hawthorne studies and other experiments demonstrated the limits of this strategy within work groups. Current experiences with complex and changing systems have raised similar doubts about the ability of control systems to coordinate adequately groups that are organizational subsystems.

Some of the chronic problems within organizations can be

viewed from the perspective of intergroup dynamics. For example, in many organizations interdepartmental cooperation and conflict are of major concern. How does one get Unit A and Unit B to mesh their efforts rather than competing and sabotaging each other? How do we promote a relationship among units which leads to open communication and problem-solving rather than game playing? Managerial strategies which aim to go beyond the futility of simply drawing new lines on the organization chart or issuing memoranda about the need for better cooperation must deal with the process issues and related factors. Interdepartmental collaboration rests on effective and open communication, shared goal setting and control, trust, and a reduction in stereotyping and politicking. This kind of relationship can be built over time by bringing members of the units together to participate in problem solving processes. In Chapter 7 we will touch on organization development techniques for helping to work on intergroup conflict.

Other classic problems of organizations can be usefully viewed as intergroup issues. For example, line/staff relationships have been discussed extensively by managers. Often there is jealousy, contesting for control and negative stereotyping between line operators who "do the work" (such as clerical or production workers) and technical or professional staff who provide control and support services (accounting, personnel, engineering).[15] Similarly, union and management relationships can be viewed as intergroup problems. In both these cases the problem is to help the opposing groups become less polarized and uncommunicative and to assist them to engage in mutual problem solving about how to move toward collaborative and mutually helpful relationships.

HUMAN NEEDS AND ORGANIZATIONAL DEMANDS

One of the ongoing debates among those interested in the human side of work is whether the demands of the organization are compatible or incompatible with the needs of its members. Or, put in terms of our present discussion, can the requirements of the six boxes be met in such a way that the organization is *effective* (the subject of our next chapter) while maintaining a climate that satisfies human needs? In earlier times when work was the curse of the common man, the answer usually was that a job was intended to provide only economic rewards. In this century, however, we have evolved a value stance that has hoped, if not demonstrated, that work can be fulfilling and need satisfying. We have sometimes gone even further and suggested that work can result in psychological growth.

In his earlier writings, Chris Argyris raised forcefully the issue of human needs versus organizational demands.[16] It was his contention that traditional hierarchical organizations, by demanding unthinking adherence to many rules and procedures, frustrate the higher level needs (as in Maslow's hierarchy) of its members—the ego and growth needs—and causes them to regress in their psychological maturity. Thus, modes of behavior that are irresponsible and immature occur because of the climate. Ways of accommodating human needs within the system need to be found if satisfaction as well as productivity are to be increased. Methods of improving the sociotechnical interaction are being developed and will be discussed in the last chapter.

A more pessimistic view of the possibility of improving the person-organization interaction is being proposed by several contemporary political and social theorists. Frederic Thayer sees hierarchy, as it shows up in "superior-subordinate" relations, as an unnatural and repressing type of interpersonal relationship. He foresees the "withering away" of traditional hierarchical forms, which will be replaced with newer, and as yet undefined, work systems.[17] These will probably involve, Thayer theorizes, small groups of a rather free-floating nature. In any event, the major need is to construct new systems that do not rely on hierarchy and control, and thus do not sacrifice the quality of the working life of the members for the gain of the organizations.

Other observers have taken a more global and culturally based view of the individual-organizational interaction. Hart and Scott point out that our society has built and manned large complex organizations because they provide us the promise of achieving happiness through material abundance.[18] The *organizational imperative* is the view that since the organization is good for people, whatever is necessary to enhance the health of the organization *should* be done. Workers have made an implicit decision to trade off sets of needs. They more-or-less willingly behave obediently toward organizational authorities, sacrificing some of their immediate individualistic needs and values in order to gain longer term economic and security payoffs. Thus, we have bought the organizational imperative as an essential aspect of our lives and have thereby assigned a lower priority to individuality, which in this chapter we refer to as higher level needs. Hart and Scott suggest that some of the alienation and social unrest of the 1960s and 1970s is a reaction against the domination of the organizational imperative.

PUBLIC AND PRIVATE SYSTEMS

It is certainly legitimate to ask whether public systems are unique in their structures and processes in ways which distinguish them from other types of organizations. The broadest answer is that it is difficult to generalize. Some public agencies look much like typical businesses. Examples are the United States General Services Administration which supplies other agencies and maintains their facilities, and the local public utilities which supply gas, water, or electricity to customers. Others, such as regulatory commissions, the State Department, and state welfare agencies are clearly unique to government. Some structural characteristics found more often in government include permeable boundaries (accessibility from outside sources, pressures, and influences), separation and poor communication between policy makers and administrators, diversity of functions, influence of boards, commissions, and regulatory bodies, size, and geographical dispersion. These structural factors often frustrate the new manager who enters government with a strong aspiration to "run the agency like a business" only to find that the uniqueness makes that impossible.

At least as important as the form of the structure is the way in which the structure comes about. The textbook prescription is that "structure follows function", you set up a particular structure to fulfill the need to perform a certain function. For example, if you find your organization needing to purchase large quantities of goods and supplies, you set up a purchasing department. In the public arena, however, structures are sometimes created for reasons other than legitimate functional needs. Visibility to voters, the need to exert greater control over a certain unit, or pressure to set up a politician's pet project may also be behind structural changes.

Once you do create a structure, it is extremely difficult to change because it tends to develop its own dependent constituency of supporters who benefit from its existence. For these reasons, reformers propose *sunset legislation* which requires that the function of a given structure be rejustified at regular intervals. Otherwise the unit automatically goes out of existence.

As for the processes of human interaction in public organizations, fewer differences probably exist. People communicate, compete, collaborate, and conflict regardless of the setting. There are, perhaps, differences of degree in some circumstances. We suggested earlier that scrutiny of the internal activities of public agencies by the media, elected officials, and various interest groups may cause communication to be more closed, conflict to be suppressed, and the climate to be more formal and protective.

CONCLUSION

Establishing an organization structure—the anatomy—staffed with qualified personnel and equipped with appropriate technology creates the potential for effective cooperative effort. Reward systems energize the system by relating to human needs, and an authority system exerts the control intended to keep behavior directed along appropriate paths. We have seen, however, that there is yet another dimension to be dealt with, that of the human interactions processes—communication, cooperation, conflicts, and so on. It is important for these processes to function in ways that are supportive of the organization's goals. The sociotechnical systems viewpoint provides a model for understanding these processes. In the following chapters we will begin to explore ways of affecting them.

NOTES TO CHAPTER 4

1. The human problems associated with these nontraditional models are discussed by Chris Argyris in "Today's Problems with Tomorrow's Organizations," *Journal of Management Studies*, vol. 4, no. 1, 1967, pp. 31-55.

Reprinted in W. B. Eddy and W. W. Burke (eds.); *Behavioral Science and the Manager's Role*, 2d ed., La Jolla, Calif.: University Associates, 1980.

2. See Eric Trist et al., *Organizational Choice*, London: Tavistock, 1963. A. K. Rice, *Productivity and Social Organization: The Ahmedabad Experiment*, London: Tavistock, 1958. W. A. Pasmore and J. J. Sherwood (eds.), *Sociotechnical Systems: A Sourcebook*, La Jolla, Calif.: University Associates, 1978.

3. Pasmore and Sherwood, op. cit., p. 3.

4. Rensis Likert, *New Patterns of Management*, New York: McGraw-Hill, 1961, p. 113.

5. The view of groups as coalitions is discussed by R. M. Cyert and J. G. March, *A Behavioral Theory of the Firms*, Englewood Cliffs, N.J.: Prentice-Hall, 1963.

6. I am indebted to Richard E. Byrd for suggesting the first part of the list of process variables. Interpretations and additions are my responsibility.

7. Chester Barnard, *The Functions of the Executive*, Cambridge, Mass.: Harvard University Press, 1938.

8. See the following for useful discussions of power: J. R. P. French, Jr., and B. Raven, "The Bases of Social Power" in D. Cartwright and A. Zander (eds.), *Group Dynamics: Research and Theory*, New York: Harper & Row, 1958. Also see David C. McClelland, *Power: The Inner Experience*, New York: Wiley-Halsted, 1975.

9. William Schutz, *FIRO. A Three Dimensional Theory of Interpersonal Behavior*, New York: Holt, Rinehart and Winston, 1958.

10. Douglas McGregor, *The Human Side of Enterprise*, New York: McGraw-Hill, 1960, Chapter 5.

11. See, for example, the *Journal of Conflict Resolution*.

12. See the work of Jack Gibb, "Defensive Communication," *Journal of Communication*, vol. 11, 1961, pp. 141-148.

13. One of the more useful treatments of trust building is Kim Giffin and R. E. Barnes, *Trusting Me, Trusting You*, Columbus, Ohio: C. E. Merrill, 1976.

14. Harlan Cleveland, *The Future Executive*, New York, Harper & Row, 1972, p. 85.

15. For an analysis of line-staff relationships as an intergroup problem see Robert T. Golembiewski, "Line-Staff Concept Revisited: An Empirical Study of Organizational Change." *Academy of Management Journal*, vol. 17, September 1974, pp. 406-417.

16. Chris Argyris, *Personality and Organization*, New York: Harper, 1957.

17. Frederic Thayer, *An End to Hierarchy! An End to Competition!*, Second edition, New York: Franklin Watts, 1981.

18. William G. Scott and David K. Hart, *Organizational America*, Boston: Houghton Mifflin, 1979.

5

Human Organizational Effectiveness

The discussion so far in this book has been largely descriptive. We have looked at human behavior in organizations in an attempt to understand *why* things happen as they do at the individual, group, and organizational levels. The next step is to move to a prescriptive phase—to talk about *how* to deal with the behavioral factors confronted by public administrators. An intermediate step between the descriptive *why* and the prescriptive *how* is to explore the topic of effectiveness. *What* is it we are trying to accomplish? What is our objective or goal? Effectiveness at the level of individual functioning and at the level of overall organizational performance is a necessary factor to pin down before we can move on to talking about action steps. No managerial action or organizational change program can be evaluated in the abstract. We have to know whether it leads to a goal or outcome or state of affairs that has been previously agreed to as indicating success or effectiveness.

WHAT IS EFFECTIVENESS?

In the final analysis, the judgment of whether an organization or a person is effective is a subjective, philosophical matter. In spite of our progress in developing rational quantitative techniques for measuring many aspects of organizations, the question of how to determine ultimate worth cannot be solved by a computer. In the private sector, profit is often used as the indicator of effectiveness, but of course it is only a partial and sometimes misleading indicator. A firm may show a short-run profit but be heading toward bankruptcy; another firm may be making money based on past ideas and accomplishment, but may not be investing anything in future developments to maintain its competitive edge; still another may be running in the black but doing so at the expense of polluting the water and air. Are these organizations effective? A stock market investor interested only in quick profits might think so. The Mayor's Council on Economic Development might have its doubts. And how about a company that makes a lot of money selling a worthless patent medicine, or a public regulatory agency that wins political support and thus greater budgets by playing ball with those whom it regulates?

Effectiveness in the public sector is even more difficult to measure. In theory, the goals and functions are set through legislation and/or by board actions of elected or appointed representatives. This is referred to as *policy*—the "What business are we in?" question raised by Weisbord's six-box model in Chapter 4. Effectiveness, then, ought to be evaluated on the basis of whether an agency performs to fulfill its policy mandates. In practice it is not so easy. Policies change to meet public wants or needs or to respond to political demands. Sometimes conflicting policies are handed down. At other times the policy statements are so broad and open-ended that it is very difficult to know whether the agency has fulfilled the policy. This leaves room for varying interpretations of the level of an agency's effectiveness and thus provides opportunities for friends to praise and enemies to criticize the same system.

It has been the tendency for each author who writes on organizations and management to provide his or her own definition of effectiveness. Many of these stem from the values of the author, what he or she thinks is good or desirable. Thus, for example, Barnard sees the central issue in organization as that of human cooperation. He says, "What we mean by effectiveness of cooperation is the accomplishment of the recognized objectives of cooperative action. The degree of accomplishment indicates the degree of effectiveness."[1]

Gortner points out that

> Legislators measure the success of government by comparing policy implementation to the original intent of the law. On the other hand, citizens measure the success of government primarily through their feelings. While they may observe the overall efficiency and effectiveness of agencies and programs, the factor that most favorably impresses the average citizen is the speed and courtesy with which their problems and complaints are handled.[2]

In a more systematic analysis, Stogdill identified the three major dimensions of achievement as *productivity, integration,* and *morale.*[3] In doing so, he asserted that there is no single indicator that captures a group's total performance. Productivity refers not only to output but also to a gain in the value of the product or service because of the functioning of the system. Integration refers to the viability of the internal structure and processes—whether the system works smoothly or encounters poor coordination, conflict, high absenteeism, and so forth. Morale is an indicator of the state of attitudes, particularly in reference to whether people feel frustrated in their efforts to reach their goals.

Other observers have pointed out that whatever other factors are suggested, *survival* is the ultimate criterion of organizational effectiveness. As it is usually presented, this position views the organization as operating in constant interaction with its environment (an open system). Its existence is contingent upon its ability to elicit support from the environment in the form of money or other resources in return for providing some goods or services. This definition, as well as most of the others, rests on an assessment of the *fit* between the organization and its environment. As we will see when we return to this topic later in the chapter, the implication of this definition is that it is important for the organization's leaders to identify the salient elements in the environment and assess their needs and demands.

Effectiveness and Efficiency

One of the more useful points related to this topic is the distinction between effectiveness and *efficiency.* Effectiveness, as we have seen, denotes the level of goal attainment, our success in doing what we have decided to do. Efficiency is quite different, although some do not appreciate the difference. Efficiency refers to the cost of doing whatever it is we do. Cost controls, preventive maintanance, personnel evaluations, and quality controls help an organization become efficient, to get more impact for their dollars. Such efficiency measures *may* contribute to effectiveness, but they are not a substitute for it. A high level of efficiency probably helped a buggy whip factory stay in business a little longer during the 1920s, but unless the firm saw to its effectiveness by reappraising and redirecting its product line its days were probably numbered. Similarly, a public agency that puts most of its attention into efficiency programs, such as fiscal controls and audits, may protect itself from criticisms of "inefficiency" from the media, but may wake up to find it has lost its political support because it no longer is relevant to the needs of its constituents.

Mixed Effectiveness Criteria

One of the confusions in government is the combining within one agency of both service and regulatory functions. Thus a state highway department is assigned the responsibilities, through the policy process, of providing smooth, safe roads wherever people want to travel and also regulating the flow of traffic with stop lights, speed limit signs, and other measures. Some of the criteria of effectiveness in each of these cases may be similar. Others may be quite different. The reduction of accidents, for example, might be an effectiveness criterion that the entire unit could relate to. On the other hand, a number of driver complaints might be a sign of poor performance by the road builders but good performance by the regulators. Such mixed criteria are almost certain to cause difficulty and require a continuous process of reevaluating and reclarifying policy.

If one is interested in doing something about effectiveness it is useful to think of three levels of analysis: individual employee effectiveness, managerial effectiveness, and organizational effectiveness. In the sections that follow we will consider these three levels and possible techniques for enhancing them.

INDIVIDUAL EFFECTIVENESS

The problem of how to assure that one's organization is populated by competent, committed, effective employees has occupied a major share of the attention of managers throughout modern times. And a good share of the mythology and folklore of management has been devoted to ideas about how to supervise in such a way as to enhance subordinates' performance. Thus the neophyte manager trainee fresh out of college may be told by one old timer, "The secret is to let 'em know who's boss right from the start." While another sage may confide, "If you can win their respect and loyalty they'll do anything you want." In search of less ambiguous and contradictory information about employee performance, organizations have established a number of programs and functions to deal with employee relations, or, in the current lingo, "human resource utilization."

Recruitment, Selection, and Placement

An obvious place to begin the effort to enhance employee effectiveness is at the initial stage. The personnel unit in most organizations has been given the task of recruiting a pool of qualified applicants for openings; selecting those most likely to perform successfully (through the use of tests, interviews, and reference checks); and placing new employees so as to maximize the match between their skills and attitudes and the requirements of the job.

In its heyday in the 1950s it was believed by its advocates that the field of personnel psychology held promise of solving many of the human problems of organizations through the development of scientific approaches to selection and placement.[4] The cornerstone of personnel psychology was testing. Sophisticated test construction and validation techniques were devised through the use of advanced statistical analysis. The federal government's Civil Service Commission (now the Office of Personnel Management) has been a leader in scientific selection techniques partly in order to upgrade the quality of federal employees and partly to fulfill the mandate to overcome favoritism and bias in hiring by selecting the "best qualified" candidates. Other governmental agencies and private firms vary in the degree to which they utilize the techniques of personnel psychology.

Although personnel psychology has proved to be a useful tool, it has not solved all the human problems of organizations for a variety of reasons. As we have already pointed out, human behavior in organizations is a result of the interaction between the attributes people bring with them (which tests and other selection devices attempt to estimate) and the characteristics of the sociotechnical system in which they function. Thus, factors not studied in the selection process may play a major role in performance. In addition, the selection devices are themselves imperfect measuring instruments that must couch their predictions in terms of probabilities. Some agencies compound the problem by purchasing highly advertised but unproven tests or tests that have not been validated for that particular agency. Other organizations make the further error of relying solely on interviews for their selection and placement in spite of the evidence that even well-trained interviewers are unreliable and inaccurate in evaluating individuals.

A recent addition to the technology of selection is the *assessment center*.[5] Rather than submitting to an hour or two of testing and interviewing, the individual being evaluated in an assessment center is put in a group of around ten other candidates for a period of time from a day to a week. A variety of group exercises, tests, and interviews is utilized with a staff assessor observing and rating the candidates. The advantages of assessment centers are that they produce a variety of measurements and observations of a candidate over a longer period of time, and through the use of group simulation exercises may obtain a more accurate picture of how the individual would function in a real situation. Although assessment centers originated in industry they have spread to government agencies, including the Peace Corps and the Internal Revenue Service. Evaluations of assessment centers indicate that they have potential for providing very useful data for selection decisions, but they are subject to the same problems as other attempts to predict human performance.

In summary, improving the employee in-take process as a way of increasing effectiveness is a useful but partial approach. Any organization that hires significant numbers of people needs a professionally run personnel unit that conducts ongoing research to evaluate and validate the techniques used. However, such an approach is only the beginning and should not be confused with a complete program of human resources utilization.

The Psychological Contract and Objective Setting

One of the factors that the traditional personnel psychology position overlooked is that the selection and placement process is a two-way transaction. At the same time the organization is evaluating the applicant, the applicant in turn is evaluating the organization as a prospective work site. Each gathers information about the other and each forms expectations about the degree to which needs are likely to be satisfied. If the candidate is offered a position and accepts it there is a contract established about such matters as salary, work hours, job assignment, and fringe benefits. These terms and mutual expectations are arrived at openly and officially.

There is another set of expectations held by each side, however, that are often not openly discussed or clearly spelled out. These expectations involve what Edgar Schein has labeled the *psychological contract*.[6]

The important thing about the psychological contract is that it demonstrates that many of the assumptions and expectations upon which employees and organizations base important actions and decisions are never overtly discussed, much less negotiated. Thus many employees know that their job description is a very general and inexact statement, but are not clear about what is really expected of them. Personnel researchers who interview a boss and his or her subordinate, asking each what are the important elements of the subordinate's job responsibilities, often get strikingly different replies. And employee satisfaction studies over the past five decades have consistently found that major sources of employee concern are not knowing what one's boss expects, what the important criteria of effectiveness are, and how one is evaluated. This lack of clarity, of course, is highly likely to have a negative impact on effectiveness as well as morale and is almost certain to constitute a source of difficulty between subordinate and boss.

The solution is to make sure that the psychological contract is openly and explicitly negotiated, with both parties stating their own expectations and their reactions to the other's expectations. In this way the chances of working at cross-purposes or on the wrong tasks are considerably lessened.

One technique that was originally designed to deal with difficulties in the psychological contract is the popular program management by objectives (MBO). As it was originally conceived by Peter Drucker and Douglas McGregor, MBO is a process of contracting between the employee and the organization, as represented by the supervisor.[7] The first stage is a series of discussions between subordinate and boss about their expectations of the employee's role and contribution to the organization. Once these have been agreed to a set of objectives for the employee's performance over a specific period of time (usually three to twelve months) is established by negotiation and mutual consent. These objectives become the criteria of effectiveness. The employee, ideally, is then evaluated on the basis of how well the objectives were met, rather than according to less objective factors such as "degree of cooperativeness" or loyalty to the organization. Thus effectiveness is clearly defined as *performance* to achieve specified objectives, and there should be a minimum of confusion about mutual expectations. (Obviously there can still be confusion about other behavior not directly related to objectives, such as how open it is safe to be in expressing one's opinion, whether units cooperate with each other, if it's okay to leave early on Friday, and so forth).

The key to a successful MBO program is a mutual negotiation process between boss and subordinate culminating in a statement of objectives that the employee understands and "owns." The employee says, "Yes, those are *my* objectives as well as the organization's, I am willing to work toward them and be evaluated according to my success in reaching them." Unfortunately, many attempts at establishing MBO programs have misunderstood or ignored the principles of contracting. They have viewed MBO as a rational planning process in which objectives are defined by upper management or consultants and are laid down more or less unilaterally for subordinates to follow. In such cases, as many disillusioned managers know, there is no contract and often no adequate understanding. Employees view the effort as "just another one of those programs management tries to foist off on us" and it dies out unless someone constantly reintroduces it.[8]

The process of psychological contracting has the further adtage of assisting with one of the chronic problems in management —that of performance evaluation. Most public agencies as well as firms have a procedure whereby the manager periodically fills out a form designed to rate the employee's effectiveness and then discuss it with the employee. In spite of the obvious need for feedback about performance, it is rare to find an organization that is satisfied with its appraisal system. Managers are uncomfortable discussing employees' weaknesses with them, rating forms contain subjective terms such as "cooperativeness" and "self-understanding" and once or twice a year is not often enough for feedback about performance. Further, there is substantial evidence that the traditional unilateral performance appraisal is not very useful in changing employee behavior in a more effective direction. The employee has little participation and thus little stake in the process, tends to remember the positive and forget the negative, and seldom gets anything from the process that is concrete and practical enough to provide much help in improving performance. The contracting model of evaluation, whether MBO or another version, is more useful because it provides for mutual participation and clearly defined objectives to be used as criteria.[9]

Training and Development

The emphasis in human resource utilization has shifted somewhat from selection (letting in only effective employees) to development (working with existing employees to help them learn how to be more effective). There are several reasons for this shift. As we explained, tests and other selection devices are helpful but imperfect predictors of performance. Changing personal and situational factors are almost certain to affect behavior. An employee who scored high on technical and mechanical skills during the hiring process may perform well until a shift in job responsibilities requires him to supervise other people. Or, an analyst may function extremely well when problems are brought to her desk for her to solve (as the tests predicted she would be) but fall apart when required to go out into the organization to identify new problems that need solving.

There are other causes for the shift to development. The traditional model of selection assumes there is a large pool of qualified prospective employees available, and one has only to skim off the "cream." This is not a valid assumption in many areas where particular skills or experience are required. Still another problem in selection is the myriad of regulations stemming from fair employment practices legislation, which places severe limitations on the use of any selection tool that might discriminate against a minority group. And finally, in a more positive vein, there has been an increasing interest in human learning and psychological growth as avenues for improving performance. Rather than sorting individuals into pigeon holes with semipermanent labels, there is a tendency to think of them as having the capacity to develop their skills in a number of different directions, depending on their interests and the needs of the organization.

Organizational training usually falls into two categories: technical skill training and training in human interaction skills. In addition, some programs that aim at affecting perceptions or attitudes are labeled "training," even though change rather than knowledge acquisition is the goal (for example, a program to sensitize employees to accident prevention). A form of training that focuses on work units or the entire organization and aims at changing work patterns as well as adding knowledge is *organization development,* or OD, which will be discussed in detail in Chapter 7.

If it is to contribute to employee and organizational effectiveness, training must grow out of a well-planned framework and not consist of a smorgasbord of courses based on the training director's pet topics or an elaborate audio-visual system offering courses nobody wants. The important questions are: Is the training program based on a careful assessment of learning needs among employees? Is the training directly related in both trainer and trainee's minds to establish effectiveness objectives? Can the trainees be evaluated by linking learning to job performance? Programs evaluated only on the basis of participant satisfaction scores or similarity to programs in another agency are likely to drift away from a work effectiveness orientation. There are a number of approaches to assessing training needs, including interviews of managers and employees, questionnaires, examination of performance records, and systematic observation. Often it is helpful to involve the potential trainees in the process, since they are the ones who ultimately will be subjected to the program and hope to profit from it. The central question is always, "What do the employees need to learn to function more effectively?"

Relating the training offerings directly to work performance is usually fairly straightforward in technical or mechanical areas (typing, programming a computer, operating a machine) but more difficult in the area of behavior and interpersonal relationships. Since more people experience difficulty in their work because of human relationship problems than because of technical inadequacies, this difficulty poses a challenge to trainers. Lectures about such topics as communication, sensitivity, and cooperation rarely have much impact on individuals who are ineffective in these areas. For this reason, trainers in the human interaction field have developed an assortment of "experiential" educational methods that seek to create a laboratory for learning by doing in the same way a chemist in a laboratory experiences what it is like to mix chemicals and study the reactions. One of the oldest experiential techniques is role-playing, in which the trainee tries out functioning in a new role and can observe the impact of his or her behavior on the other players and on himself or herself. Other experiential approaches to learning about human behavior include group problem-solving exercises, video taping, and analyzing interviews or other interactions, and various "games" designed to simulate real problems.

T-group training (sometimes referred to as sensitivity training) utilizes a less structured experiential approach to helping trainees better understand the many facets of human interaction.[10] In a T-group (T stands for training) ten to twelve participants meet with a consultant or facilitator for a period of several days without a specific agenda except to build the group into a small social system (very much as we defined the term earlier) that will assist them in their "learning by doing." The activities and interactions of each group serve as its own text material for that group's discussion. T-group training has been extensively evaluated and has been found to be a useful tool for enhancing interpersonal effectiveness in situations in which the participant's organization is supportive of the values and methods of the T-group, and when the training is conducted by a capable consultant. Perhaps T-group training's most significant function is that it serves as a vehicle for the installation of a broader program of organization development.

Before leaving the topic of training, one cautionary note. All too often organizations attempt to use training to deal with problems not related to skill or knowledge deficiencies, but rather to other dysfunctions in the sociotechnical system. For example, I was once asked to conduct supervisory training programs for an organization in which upper management complained, "The supervisors aren't supervising!" It was assumed that if the supervisors knew more about supervision—the principles and techniques—they would function more effectively. A diagnostic phase utilizing interviews and questionnaires was conducted prior to providing any training. The supervisors had a different view. They felt they knew the principles of supervision, but that they were not being allowed to supervise. Their roles were defined in such a way that they had little to do with employee evaluations and rewards. The personnel section had taken over many of their functions and they were often not involved in decisions having to do with their own subordinates and the work in their units. The employees were well aware of these conditions and took them as a sign that supervisors were not powerful figures. No amount of additional supervisory training would have improved the situation. On the contrary, it may well have made things worse by raising and then frustrating supervisors' hopes for improvements. This kind of misguided application of training is all too frequent. Such tactics may be used to build loyalty (that is, convince employees to work harder or more diligently), to build teamwork (convince employees to stop fighting), or to improve communication (convince employees to stop covering up the truth in order to protect themselves). While all of these are legitimate problems to be solved, it is highly unlikely that training, at least the traditional type of training, will be of much help. The danger signal is when someone says, "If only the employees would feel differently or see things differently, we could operate more smoothly. Maybe we need some training."

116 Public Organization Behavior and Development

The Work Environment and Effectiveness

Another group of factors that significantly influences employee effectiveness is the *climate* or the social psychological characteristics of the work environment. We have earlier discussed the concept of the sociotechnical system and the ways in which human variables interact with the policies, procedures, technologies, and so forth. It is part of the manager's job to understand the impact of various climatic factors on performance and to eliminate or reduce them when they are possible negative factors. In this section we will review some of the climatic factors that have been found to be related to level of effectiveness.

Of course, the idea that various aspects of the work environment affect performance is not new. Herzberg, as we noted in Chapter 3, distinguished between intrinsic and extrinsic factors. He pointed out that extrinsic factors (involving such variables as pay, working conditions, and regulations) were likely to be negative influences, while intrinsic factors (such as achievement and recognition and interesting work) usually have a more positive influence.[11]

Trist has recently suggested a similar list of job properties that relate to human needs (see Table 5-1). The assumption is that if these need areas are not satisfied, the worker-organization interface in the sociotechnical system will function unsatisfactorily, and the quality of the worker's experience as well as the quality of work will suffer.[12]

It would be highly desirable to be able to hand the manager a list of all the work climate factors that significantly affect effectiveness and say, "See that these are taken care of, and the impact of the climate will be positive." Unfortunately, the state of the art has not reached that point. However, organizational researchers have been busy studying the factor of climate and generated some interesting results. Payne and Pugh conducted a comprehensive review of the research literature on climate and summarize the results of many studies.[13] They point out that it is not always possible to clearly separate the areas of structure and climate, and that some of the climate measures are subjective in that they reflect feelings and perceptions of employees, rather than measurable

Human Organizational Effectiveness 117

Table 5-1 Properties of Jobs Related to Human Needs

Extrinsic	Intrinsic
Fair and adequate pay	Variety and challenge
Job security	Continuous learning
Benefits	Discretion, autonomy
Safety	Recognition and support
Health	Meaningful social contribution
Due process	Desirable future

characteristics. My tallying and consolidating of the climate factors reported by Payne and Pugh reveals the following list, some of which overlap:

Organizational Climate Factors

1. *Individual Autonomy.* Degree to which employees are allowed freedom to choose how they do their jobs.
2. *Degree of Structure.* Degree to which organizational functioning is tightly prescribed and defined.
3. *Reward Orientation.* Degree to which rewards for performance are positive, appropriate and significant.
4. *Orientation to Development and Progressiveness.* Degree to which support is given for training, human growth, and organizational change.
5. *Consideration and Support.* Degree of warmth, support empathy provided by the organization, as experienced by employees.
6. *Concentration of Authority.* Degree to which authority and decision making are centralized and controlled by a few persons.
7. *Risk-Taking.* Do employees feel safety and support and thus feel enabled to try new things?
8. *Cohesiveness and Morale.* Is there a feeling of belonging and loyalty, characterized by low absenteeism and low turnover?
9. *Openness of Communication.* Are messages accurately and easily sent throughout the organization?
10. *Stratification.* Is the organization characterized by many rigid hierarchical layers?

118 Public Organization Behavior and Development

11. *Flexibility.* Are practices and procedures easy to adapt and change?
12. *Goal Clarity.* Are goals and performance criteria clearly and objectively defined?
13. *Conflict.* Is there unresolved disagreement and hostility?
14. *Use of Control Data.* Are performance reports (accounting data, production reports, etc.) used for punishment or to allow self-correction?
15. *Task Specialization.* Are tasks narrowly and rigidly prescribed for employees?
16. *Hindrances.* Feeling by workers that they are burdened by routine duties and that the organization does not facilitate their work.
17. *Heterogeneity.* Degree to which members are different and perhaps polarized in their views, values, or needs.
18. *Maturity.* Degree to which the group has gained the experience to take a good deal of responsibility for its performance.
19. *Integration.* Degree to which individuals mesh their efforts and work smoothly together.

Since this list is a result of one person's consolidation of the brief summaries of dozens of studies, it must be thought of as illustrative only. Though many of the factors show up in similar forms in several studies, another observer might compile a somewhat different list. Further, it needs to pointed out that clear-cut relationships between climate factors and effectiveness are not always found to be present. Thus one needs to be careful when operating prescriptively with the climate research. For example, while it is probably safe to suggest that a positive reward system, supportive climate, high morale, cohesiveness, flexibility, and open communication are likely to contribute to a more effective organization, some of the other factors could be either positive, negative, or neutral, depending upon the other aspects of the situation. For example, high autonomy, low structure, decentralization, and high risk-taking might contribute greatly to effectiveness in a research and development unit, but be counterproductive in a finance and budget operation. In addition, since there is an uncertain relationship between productivity and satisfaction, some factors might, in some situations, lead to better feelings but not greater effectiveness. Nevertheless, a manager could do worse than to run through the list of nineteen factors and evaluate his or her unit's function on each. At the very least, such an analysis would be a worthwhile exercise in applying social science concepts to organizational analysis.

Task Design and Effectiveness

The way an employee or manager's job is defined and structured also has a significant impact on the effectiveness with which it is performed. Plato, Weber, Henry Ford, and many others felt that *specialization* is the key to effectiveness. Teach a person how to do a few things very well, limit the job to those few things, and have him or her perform them over and over.

Frederick Taylor used scientific methods to implement the idea of specialization and became the father of scientific management. However, Taylor's idea went beyond specialization to the physiological aspects of test performance. He looked into the efficiency of various kinds of hand motions, tool designs, materials arrangements, and seating positions. His scientifically designed combinations of tasks could be performed with the least wasted motion, least fatigue, in the least time. As we noted earlier in the book, Taylor's idea was to derive effectiveness from efficiency by offering workers bonuses for high levels of output. Taylor's legions of stopwatch-carrying efficiency experts, industrial engineers, and human engineers descended on organizations amidst a debate about "whether you engineer the job for the man, or the man for the job."

The growing popularity of the human relations movement slowed down the scientific management movement somewhat, at least among theorists if not in actual practice. Narrow, unstimulating tasks, it was felt, dehumanize workers, turn them into robots, sap the organization and its employees of effectiveness. Overspecialization risked a "brave new world" of overcontrolled humans. HEW's *Work in America* study lent credence to the suspicions with the revelation of the "blue collar blues," which showed disturbing numbers of workers turned off to their jobs (and perhaps turned on to drugs).[14]

Now, just when a five-acre farm in Alaska has seemed the only alternative to a narrow, boring job, the gear is turning again. Task design is assuming a more important role in organizational effectiveness programs, but with a different focus than Taylor's.

Before describing the current developments, it may be useful to describe the background of the field. As sometimes happens in applied science, a solid foundation has been laid which supports the new thrust. For several decades personnel and industrial psychologists have been developing the field of job and task analysis. Careful studies have been done in many organizations that provide a fairly well-developed technology for analyzing the basic dimensions for jobs and also useful catalogs of job components. Thus when social scientists set out to "improve" jobs for workers they had an array of useful tools to deal with.

The current focus on work redesign, popularly called *quality of working life* (QWL), derives from at least two schools of thought. One group of innovators began their work at the Tavistock Institute in Great Britain. Working in the coal mining industry and several other organizations, they studied the relationships between people and their work, developed the concept of the sociotechnical system, and began experiments in the redesign of jobs and tasks with the goal of finding ways to make them less dull and stultifying. Eric Trist, one of the leaders in the QWL movement, has stated

> The problem is not simply that of either "adjusting" people to technology or technology to people; it consists of organizing the man-machine interface so that the best match can be obtained between both. Rather it is essential that the whole socio-technical system—of which both technologies and humans are parts—be effectively "optimized." This is necessary at all levels and in all types of technology: the "mediating" technologies with which the service industries are concerned, the intensive technologies with which professionals and R&D organizations are concerned, as well as the "long linked" technologies which form the basis of manufacturing. The task, in essence, is one of joint optimization.[15]

Field research projects in Europe and the United States have experimented with ways of redesigning tasks and overall jobs (combinations of tasks) in order not only to improve efficiency but also employee satisfaction and effectiveness. A commonly cited example is the Volvo plant in Sweden in which the traditional assembly line with its narrow and repetitive jobs has been replaced with work teams who build an entire automobile and may switch and recombine tasks over the course of a day.

A parallel and related technique is job enrichment advocated by motivational psychologist Frederick Herzberg, industrial trainer Robert Ford, and others.[16] You may recall from Chapter 3 that it is Herzberg's view that many jobs contain too few of the intrinsic satisfiers—achievement, recognition, interesting work. Attempts to substitute extrinsic rewards such as pay, fringe benefits, and better working conditions have negligible and short-term effects for many workers. The key to greater satisfaction and productivity is perceived to be enriched jobs—jobs that contain more tasks that are more interesting and challenging and provide more opportunity to assume responsibility.

One approach to improving working life as well as productivity is the *quality circle* (sometimes called quality control circle). Quality circles are small groups of employees who meet regularly to discuss and solve problems that occur in their sector of the organization. A program at the Norfolk Naval Shipyard demonstrates the concept's applicability to governmental operations. At the Norfolk Shipyard the project began with nine circles composed of twelve to twenty workers each. Machinists, electricians, riggers, engineering technicians and others met weekly to attempt to resolve problems that hampered quality and productivity and caused frustration. Participation is voluntary and the agency provides a facilitator, eight hours of training for members and a guarantee to listen to the circles' suggestions.

One circle came up with a solution to a chronic problem, that of standing in long lines to obtain tools. The circle studied and documented the problem and handed management a proposed solution which changed the arrangements for handing out tools and the record keeping system. Average waiting time was reduced from twelve to five minutes, two computers were eliminated and a saving of over $200,000 was achieved. Both employees and management show enthusiasm about the much higher level of employee participation and plans are under way to expand the program to thirty-six circles.[17]

In Chapter 7, where the focus will be on the strategies for

improving public systems, we will describe in greater detail some of the possible applications of the advanced techniques of task and work design.

The Formal Reward System

The use of money in the form of wages, bonuses, fringe benefits, and piece-rate incentives has traditionally been viewed as the avenue to increasing employee productivity. Traditional strategies for getting workers to follow scientifically designed tasks was to reward them for the increased output they would attain by utilizing the new methods. Recent theorists, backed by a good deal of research, have cast doubt on the value of money as the prime motivator it was once thought to be. Job satisfaction surveys frequently show good wages ranking fourth or fifth on workers' priority lists, after such items as feeling in on things, being appreciated for accomplishments, understanding, and security.[18] Experiences as far back as the Hawthorne studies of the 1920s and 1930s have demonstrated that group social pressures sometimes act to offset and neutralize the positive effects of piece-rate incentives. And many is the manager who has found out the hard way that complaints about wages are often masks that cover up other dissatisfactions.

The reasons for money's imperfection as an incentive for productivity are understandable through the theories of motivation we discussed earlier. McGregor pointed out twenty years ago that since needs once satisfied are no longer motivators of behavior, it is invalid to expect employees of large modern organizations to be motivated primarily by economic factors.[19] Their "lower level" physiological and safety needs are often fairly well satisfied; it is the social and egoistic needs—the needs for association, support, self-esteem, achievement, recognition, and so on, that are most potent. Thus money as a pure economic motivator is of limited value. Herzberg arrived at a view of incentives that is compatible with that of McGregor in his finding that pay is a hygiene factor—the cause of a good deal of dissatisfaction, but rarely a force in positive, longer term motivation.

Another demonstration of the problems of attempting to use money as a motivator to achieve effectiveness comes through the attempts to link performance appraisal with economic rewards. In a series of major studies at General Electric, Meyer, Kay, and French found that the practice of conducting appraisal interviews for the dual purposes of (1) getting the employee to correct his/her behavior and (2) establishing a salary level was ineffective.[20] Only by disconnecting the salary decision from the regular evaluation discussion and focusing on goal-setting was it possible to derive any improved performance from the program. The possibility of gaining or losing money appeared to confuse the discussion of positive and negative elements of performance.

The possibilities for using salary as an incentive are not all negative, however. Hammer conducted an extensive review of research on merit systems and concluded that major problems with many programs are that they are poorly administered and supported and that often there is not a clear linkage demonstrated between performance and pay.[21] This may be because raters are biased or ineffective, rewards are inequitable or the appraisal situation is threatening to employees. There is evidence that it is possible to design merit systems in which there is a clear and demonstrable relationship between productivity and pay, and such systems can affect productivity. However, pay cannot in this day and age buy control, make employees feel good about dull and dead-end work, or compensate for a negative, unhealthy climate.

Lawler, a leading student of the impact of pay upon performance and effectiveness, agrees that pay can be a significant motivational force, though not the only one.[22] It is useful to consider that the pay system is only one part of the broader organizational system. Thus financial rewards do not operate alone, but interact with other dynamics of the organization, including its management style, trust level, and history of the pay program. In order to know what changes in the pay system would be likely to improve productivity it is necessary to diagnose a number of things about the situation: employees' expectations, and the importance they attach to pay, perceived fairness of present system, management's openness to employee participation in decision making, to name a few.

Lawler describes some new approaches to pay administration that hold promise of improving both productivity and quality of work life. The new approaches include: (1) cafeteria fringe benefit programs, in which employees are given a lump sum to allocate as they wish across the available health, insurance, and retirement programs; (2) skill evaluation plans in which employees are compensated on the basis of the numbers of different jobs they learn to do, rather than the job they happen to be doing at the time; (3) lump-sum salary increases, in which a yearly increase can be taken all at once or spread out, depending on the employee's choices and needs, and (4) more openness about pay rates and wider participation in pay policies and decisions about individual rates of pay. Such techniques are being tried out in various organizations and hold promise of improving the value of pay in increasing productivity.

A final approach to compensation needs mentioning. It has been noted for some years that there are major problems with individual piece-rate incentive systems—quite apart from the question of whether money is a good motivator. The problems include the fact that individual incentive programs often pit workers against each other in competitive battles about not only who produces the most, but also who gets the fastest assignments, the best materials, and the best machines. Individually oriented programs also discourage cooperation and do little to encourage employee commitment to the goals and needs of the overall organization. For these reasons group incentive plans have been developed. These plans operate on the premise that if you provide an incentive for all the employees in an organization to contribute cost saving and productivity increases, and reward all of them in relation to their regular salary, the chances of a cooperative and mutually supportive effort will be increased. The most widely used and best researched of the participative group incentive plans is the Scanlon plan, first developed during the depression of the 1930s by union leader Joe Scanlon who sought a way for employees to assist in the revival of a financially troubled company. The plan involves an interlocking series of worker-management committees, an open suggestion system for generating ideas about cost saving and productivity improvement, and a monthly bonus if certain financial criteria are met. Evaluation research indicates that in settings in which it can be applied, the Scanlon plan can make a significant contribution to effectiveness.[23]

Although there is no unanimity about the relationship between pay and effectiveness, it is possible to sort out some general principles from the foregoing material that should provide a fairly safe approach to pay administration. Pay is important, but not *the* only incentive, and often not the most important. Pay can clearly have a negative effect on morale and performance when it is seen as inadequate or inequitable, or is used as a threat in evaluation situations. It can have a positive effect when employees expect and value the amount of the reward they will receive, and when it is symbolic of other needs such as recognition, status, and security. Pay cannot usually be counted on to erase the toll of dull, uninspiring work, unpleasant management, or attempts to manipulate. There is probably a good deal to be said for making the pay system less closed and tightly controlled and encouraging employees to participate more. Badly conceived evaluation and reward programs seem to be at least partly responsible for the poor showing of pay as an incentive for effectiveness.

The public manager will have to sort out for himself or herself the applicability of the above ideas to the specific agency. It is no secret that so-called merit systems have not always worked well in public agencies. Attempts to differentiate between high and low producers often break down because of fuzzy criteria or unwilling managers. Tenure and not making enemies sometimes become substitutes for effectiveness, and almost everyone may get a "merit" raise just for keeping regular hours.

One problem for public managers is that often they do not have full control of the pay system. Wage levels, fringe benefits, promotion criteria, and other policies may be set by legislative bodies, and appointed commissions may oversee the administration of personnel policies. Under these circumstances, a program to use monetary incentives requires careful planning and liaison. Nigro and Nigro describe several cases in which state and local governments have developed ways of paying bonuses for individual or group performance. City water-meter readers earn extra pay above a set base rate for extra task accomplishment and state office workers operate on a piece-work compensation plan based on handling cases. Supervisors may be rewarded on the basis of cost reduction or the overall productivity of their employees.[24]

Under the Civil Service Reform Act of 1978, federal agencies have the opportunity to pay differential rewards. Senior-level executives (GS 16 to 18 and certain other top positions) may be awarded bonuses for outstanding contributions. Middle managers (GS 13 to 15) will receive *merit pay*. Under this plan one-half the funds available for pay increases will be paid as an adjustment to individuals' wages to make them more comparable to industrial levels. The other half will be divided among employees in a unit on the basis of merit. The criteria for demonstrating merit involve establishing performance standards for every job, with an opportunity for employee input, and evaluating level of performance on important elements. This system is too new to have been evaluated at this writing. Perhaps the most significant thing about its enactment is the demonstration of consensus among administrators, politicians, and personnel specialists that financial incentive could be a useful device for motivating employees toward effective performance.

Dealing with Ineffective Employees

There are, unfortunately, times when the problem is not how to raise and sustain the performance levels of average employees, but rather what to do about the employee who consistently falls into the "ineffective" category. Ineffectiveness, of course, is a very general term, but usually denotes a failure on the part of the individual to come up to some standard of performance in productivity, attendance, social compatibility, or other areas deemed significant. In my experience, attempting to cope with the ineffective employee is one of management's most troublesome activities, but one on which the social sciences have provided relatively little assistance. When midcareer managers in my classes are asked to write cases about managerial problems, a high percentage invariably write about the "problem employee" who performs below standard, causes friction in the office, can't be depended on, but seems immune to performance evaluations, warnings, threats, counseling, and pleading. The problem may also include alcoholism, drugs, absenteeism, emotional instability, or accident proneness.

One of the reasons the ineffective employee is so difficult to change is that the behavior, like other dysfunctional social behavior such as delinquency or corruption, usually stems from a complex of factors, not a single cause. Further, these factors may have been operating for years, making it unrealistic to expect quick changes. Too often a single established procedure is used to attempt to deal with all cases of ineffectiveness—a pink warning slip, a stern discussion with the supervisor, or a trip to the personnel department, all of these perhaps based on the assumption that the employee is intentionally malingering and could do much better if he or she really tried. Unfortunately, such techniques may serve primarily to raise the stress level and further lower, rather than raise, effectiveness.

Miner, who has specialized in studying ineffective performance, proposes a control model for dealing with it.[25] The first stage is a diagnostic one in which the cause(s) are determined. Several lists of possible causal factors have been developed, and these can be used as a check list. The lists consist of factors similar to those we are discussing in this chapter: *individual characteristics*, such as skills, knowledge, emotional factors, stress level, motivation, physical condition; *personal life and societal elements*, such as family factors and social groups; *levels of education and training; factors in the work environment and climate;* and *organizational and management issues*, such as clarity of objectives, quality of supervision, design of the job, the reward system. Most frequently ineffectiveness is the result of an unsuccessful interaction between individual characteristics and situational forces, possibly complicated by outside family and societal factors.

Only when the crucial causal factors have been identified can a strategy for resolving them be devised. In my experience a common error is that the manager too quickly tries out a solution before a cause has been determined. Miner proposes training courses to help managers deal with ineffective performers. Studies indicate that such courses can be helpful for supervisors who often feel, "I'm not a psychiatrist, how am I going to be of any help to the person?"

Firing is, of course, one solution to ineffective performance. However, given the many legal and collective-bargaining constraints, the high cost of replacement, and the possibility that a newly hired person may not perform any better, other options also need to be looked at. Which ones are to be used, again, depends upon the sources of the problem. Goal clarification (objective setting and drawing up the psychological contract), counseling, coaching, penalties, a change in assignments, job redesign, training, changes in management style, and modification of rewards are among the possibilities. And the reality is that because of the difficulties of changing individuals, many of the outcomes are likely to be only partial successes.

Summary: Individual Effectiveness

Thus far we have discussed some of the more significant of the many elements that affect individual effectiveness. We have looked at initial selection and placement, at understanding of and commitment to goals, training and development, the social psychological climate, task design, tangible rewards, and the special problems of ineffectiveness. These lists comprise many opportunities as well as several problems. Although some of the responsibility for dealing with strategies for effectiveness belongs to legislators, or other outside bodies, the manager is most directly involved and has the most impact role—or should have. It is to the topic of managerial effectiveness that we turn next.

MANAGERIAL EFFECTIVENESS

It is obvious to most people that, in addition to a staff of effective employees, organizational effectiveness also depends upon effective managers. Capable and committed employees can be misdirected, alienated, angered, or driven away by an incompetent manager. And, in contrast, a group of average employees can be helped to become more effective by a capable and concerned supervisor. Football teams change coaches when they lose too many games, corporations fire the president when the profit picture deteriorates, and public agencies frequently get new heads, either through elections or new appointments. It is reasonable to assume that since the leader is *responsible* for everything that goes on in his or her unit, one good way of improving what goes on is to improve (change) the leadership. In his six-box model (Chapter 4) Weisbord refers to leadership as the function that keeps the other activities in balance. Most other observers assign equally central importance to both the processes of management and the styles and skills of the individuals who inhabit the managerial roles.

Since leadership and management constitute an important field of study of their own, we have devoted the next chapter to that topic and will not dwell on it here. It is relevant to point out in the present context, however, that management's role as perceived by itself and others both inside and outside the system, may or may not place great emphasis on effectiveness. Management in some agencies is expected to keep things calm and free from public notice. In others it does the bidding of political figures. In still others its role is to fulfill certain laws or regulations at minimum cost or keep the paper flowing. Or a managerial role may be only the next step on the promotion ladder for those who perform their technical jobs well. None of these seems very effective.

Part of the push for professional management, as demonstrated in the city manager movement, the Federal Executive Service, certain state governments such as California, and the National Association of Schools of Public Affairs and Administration, is to create a set of values about effectiveness that help the manager see beyond the pressures in his or her particular agency. Thus, while we usually assume that management is the key instrument for achieving effectiveness, it must be noted that in reality management is a force that can be utilized to achieve several different ends—including, by the way, its own preservation. Thus, management effectiveness is not necessarily the same thing as organizational effectiveness. And, furthermore, a highly competent, professional manager may or may not be successful in a given setting. However, we like to think that in most agencies, managerial competence is a desirable commodity, and in Chapter 7 we will examine the styles, skills, and techniques that managers use to influence and change organizations.

THE EFFECTIVE ORGANIZATION

We now return to questions raised at the beginning of the chapter. How does an organization achieve overall effectiveness? And how do we determine what effectiveness is and how to measure it so that we'll know whether the organization is effective?

It is important to remind ourselves that the ultimate effectiveness of large-scale organizations is a matter of philosophy, public policy, and subjective judgment. Is the U.S. Department of Health and Human Services effective? Is it of marginal effectiveness, average effectiveness, or great effectiveness? Is it more or less effective than its predecessor, the Department of Health, Education, and Welfare? These questions are unanswerable in an absolute, final, objective sense. The answers depend upon one's philosophy of social service, the criteria one selects for making the judgment, which definition of the objectives of HEW one uses, what other agencies it is compared to, and other factors. One observer may view the agency as a highly effective mechanism for income redistribution—channeling federal income tax dollars to the less affluent segments of society. Within such a view, perhaps, is the belief that the inefficiencies are relatively minor and predictable for an organization of such size. Another evaluator, who believes that the criteria for evaluation should emphasize elimination of social problems such as hunger, illiteracy, and unwanted pregnancies, will doubtless come up with a different assessment, as will a representative from a tax reduction committee.

The same principle holds true for virtually every public agency, including such basic units as the animal control office (dog catcher), community hospital, or bus system. A great deal of the political debate at all levels of government actually involves varying perceptions of the effectiveness of agencies and their programs and officials. Usually each candidate behaves as though his or her views or values represent the only true reality and as though the opponent is ignoring, covering up, or lying about the truth. Rarely is there owning up to the possibility of differing perceptions based on varying values and vantage points (unless it is pointed out by the press).

In the public sector, policy implementation is as widely used an indicator of effectiveness as is profit in the private sector. (Does the National Aeronautics and Space Administration put a man on the moon? Does the city health department get all school children immunized?) In a fascinating applied research project, Pressman and Wildavsky studied the implementation of a major urban employment and construction project in Oakland, California.[26] Theirs is a saga of (to quote their subtitle) "How Great Expectations in Washington Are Dashed in Oakland." Almost everything that could have gone wrong did go wrong (true to Murphy's Law). Even with reasonably straightforward goals (to reduce minority unemployment by federally financed economic development), general agreement on philosophy, and availability of funds, the project floundered. There are several problems with using policy implementation as the indicator of effectiveness. Policies are formulated and enacted by legislative bodies comprised of individuals of differing views, incomplete information, and vested interests. Therefore they can be ambiguous, unattainable, and changing. This dilemma has contributed to the breaking down of the traditional barriers between policy and administration. Managers who are to be evaluated on the basis of policy implementation cannot afford not to try to inject notes of reality into the policy process, or to seek clarification of ambiguous sections, or influence the amount of funds allocated for a program.

As we indicated earlier, the difficulties of establishing, measuring, and evaluating operational policy effectiveness have led to emphasis on efficiency as a substitute criterion. It is common practice to enquire about whether an agency wastes funds, lends cars to employees for private use, or violates secret bidding procedures rather than asking questions about whether the agency is accomplishing well what it is supposed to be accomplishing. Although the need for efficiency is important in its own right, it is at most a contribution to effectiveness, and not a substitute for it.

In some cases, when the good of the public being served gets sacrificed for other outcomes, even efficiency can be a two-edged sword. Some of the most embarassing cases in public administration involve efficiently run failures: new high rise public housing projects that people refuse to live in, freeways which bisect and destroy stable neighborhoods, law enforcement agencies twisted toward surveillance of the political opposition. An efficient public organization in the hands of those with narrow or self-serving goals can be more a menace than a servant of the people.

Management authority Peter Drucker examines factors influencing the ineffectiveness of service institutions (a category that includes government agencies, schools, health care systems, and other nonbusiness institutions).[26] Drucker reviews three popular explanations for ineffectiveness (1) service institutions are not businesslike (that is, they are not *efficient*), (2) they are not able to attract good people, (3) their goals are too intangible and too ambiguous to focus their activities. Drucker asserts that these excuses are myths and half-truths. They do not fit service institutions any better than they fit some businesses, and, furthermore, a number of service institutions are highly effective operating under the three limitations. He contends that the only significant difference between businesses and service institutions is the way they are paid. Businesses (except for monopolies) are paid by customers in exchange for providing some desired goods or services. Public service institutions are usually paid by budget allocation out of tax revenues. Thus the relationship between effectiveness and income is more indirect and long term. Performance in a service institution is measured by budget size, which is based on promises (we will do so-and-so with the money) rather than on results. This condition creates a great temptation to avoid facing up to effectiveness (goal accomplishment) and, instead, to strategize for ways of increasing one's budget.

To avoid this problem Drucker recommends a series of steps that lean heavily on his management by objectives principles. These steps are

——A clear definition of the agency's function(s), including resolution of conflicting definitions. (This is the policy issue inherent in Weisbord's "What business are we in?" question.)
——The establishment of specified goals and objectives based on the definition of function.
——The setting of operational priorities and performance standards and the means to measure these objectively.
——A system of evaluating results and terminating objectives and programs that prove ineffective, that is, do not contribute adequately to the agency's functions.

Thus, Drucker joins other authorities who see one of the major problems as a gradual drift away from the initial major functions into other activities that may be more rewarding for the individual members. The term *goal displacement* has been used to describe this process. A federal agency created to monitor and control a field of businesses gradually drifts into a stance in which there is more comradeship than control in the relationship. An executive in another agency enhances his own career and promotion possibilities by building his unit's budget to ever greater size by seeking new projects to pursue, even though many have little to do with the unit's original function. Or the manager of a social service agency finds the goals fuzzy and difficult to focus on, so rather than pushing for clearer objectives, she settles for indicators of *efficiency*—number of case loads handled per staff member, cost of disbursing benefits, costs of travel, and so on.

As these examples indicate, there is a strong human element in the search for organization effectiveness. One of the major problems is the old dilemma of balancing personal goals and organizational goals. It is one thing to establish the function and goals of an agency by legislation and quite another to get employees to override their own personal needs to pursue the organization's goals. If there is not a good *psychological contract*, if there is not a mutually satisfactory integration of personal and organizational needs, effectiveness is hampered. At the nonmanagerial and nonsupervisory level effectiveness and efficiency are hampered by absenteeism, turnover, low effort, waste, and all the other symptoms of an unproductive climate. At managerial and professional levels the impact of a bad contract may involve the twisting of organizational goals and functions.

A Process Model of Organizational Effectiveness

Steers proposes an approach to the study of organizational effectiveness that combines a number of the elements we have discussed.[28] He conceives of organizations as open systems that utilize human performance as they seek to optimize their goals. The use of the term *goal optimization* is significant because it defines effectiveness as the organization's ability to reach realistic goals within the many constraints with which it has to work— money, technology, laws, personnel, and so on. The *maximum* goal would be an ideal or ultimate end result, whereas the *optimum* goal is the realistic level of attainment.

In the organization's goal-optimization efforts, four areas of activity contribute. These are (1) organizational characteristics, (2) environmental characteristics, (3) employee characteristics, and

Table 5-2 Factors Contributing to Organizational Effectiveness

Organizational characteristics	Environmental characteristics	Employee characteristics	Managerial policies and practices
Structure	*External*	*Organizational attachment*	Strategic goal setting
Decentralization	Complexity		Resource acquisition and utilization
Specialization	Stability	Attraction	Creating a performance environment
Formalization	Uncertainty	Retention	
Span of control		Commitment	Communication processes
Organization size	*Internal (climate)*		
Work-unit size		*Job performance*	Leadership and decision making
	Achievement orientation		
Technology	Employee centeredness	Motives, goals, and needs	Organizational adaptation and innovation
Operations		Abilities	
Materials	Reward-punishment orientation	Role clarity	
Knowledge	Security vs. risk		
	Openness vs. defensiveness		

Source: Richard M. Steers, *Organizational Effectiveness: A Behavioral View.* (Santa Monica, Calif., Goodyear, 1977).

(4) managerial policies and practices. Table 5-2 shows these four areas and their subcategories.

Each area of Table 5-2 provides both opportunities and limitations, and each area also encompasses many of the factors we have discussed previously. The organizational characteristics, as Steers defines them, are structural and technological. Both may be the subject of interventions such as reorganization and modernization in an effort to improve effectiveness. Environment refers to both internal and external factors. The conditions of complexity, stability-instability, and uncertainty are familiar in the lives of most public administrators. Employee characteristics include what we have referred to as process variables, such as commitment, and also individual psychological attributes, such as motives. Finally, managerial policies and practices describe the bag of tools the manager may use to try to engineer the system into a better position to optimize its goal-seeking effectiveness.

To the extent that Steers's listing is complete—and as a synthesis of others' research, it seems quite complete—it provides a useful overview of all the considerations necessary for managing an organization toward greater effectiveness. It is a useful companion to Weisbord's six-box model in helping the manager develop a workable schema for understanding, analyzing, and influencing the functioning of the organization.

The Adaptive-Coping Cycle

Most public managers perceive that their agencies are more interdependent with the external environment than are other organizations. They are conceived, funded, regulated, evaluated, and judged by outside forces. For this reason, Edgar Schein's *adaptive-coping cycle* is an appropriate view of effectiveness with which to conclude this chapter.[29] It is his view that organizations often fail because they do not adapt adequately to changes in the internal or external environment. Thus, for example, a public system that plods methodically along yesterday's pathways, not noticing or appreciating crucial changes in constituent values, social issues, pressure group allegiances, or other environmental realities, will soon be coping ineffectively. Furthermore, it may not notice or own up to its own ineffectiveness until external agents demand an accounting. According to Schein, the six stages in the adaptive-coping cycle are:

1. Sensing a change in some part of the internal or external environment.
2. Importing the relevant information about the change into those parts of the organization that can act upon it.
3. Changing production or conversion processes inside the organization according to the information obtained.
4. Stabilizing internal changes while reducing or managing undesired by-products (undesired changes in related systems that have resulted from the desired changes).
5. Exporting new products, services, and so on, which are more in line with the originally perceived changes in the environment.
6. Obtaining feedback on the success of the change through further sensing of the state of the external environment and the degree of integration of the internal environment.

Thus Schein reaffirms the concept of the open sociotechnical system, which interacts with its environment and seeks to bring its internal subsystems into balance with the demands placed on it. The problems of organizational effectiveness, according to Schein, have to do with failures in one or more of the six stages. The model also emphasizes that success in *all* six areas is essential; a breakdown in any one of them can stymie the total system's ability to cope.

Schein also presents his views on the internal organizational conditions necessary for effective coping to occur. These conditions are:

——The ability to take in and communicate information reliably and validly
——Internal flexibility and creativity to make changes indicated by the information obtained
——Integration and commitment to the organization's goals
——An internal climate of support and freedom from threat, since threat stifles communication and flexibility and stimulates self-protection

In Schein's view, such conditions require much more than short-term programs and structures. They rest on the basic competence, commitment, willingness to collaborate, and goal-setting efficacy of the organization's members.

CONCLUSION

We have traced the many facets of the concept of organizational effectiveness from broad value questions to narrower individual factors and back again to broader questions of overall systems performance. It is clear that there is no single criterion of effectiveness—except possibly long-term survival—which can be applied to all organizations. It is also evident that policy implementation, the standard indicator of effectiveness in government, represents a limited view. Steers's notion of goal optimization presents one of the more useful ways of thinking about effectiveness: "Can the organization achieve a level of goal attainment which is desired but realistic within the limits imposed by its various constraints and resource limitations?"

Regardless of the definition one chooses, it is obvious that overall organizational effectiveness can only be sustained by effective and well-coordinated members and subsystems and a climate that sustains nondefensive problem solving.

The other set of factors required for organizational effectiveness, according to many observers, is a cadre of managers skilled in leadership and administrative functions. It is to this topic we turn in the next chapter.

NOTES TO CHAPTER 5

1. Chester Barnard, *The Functions of the Executive*, Cambridge, Mass.: Harvard University Press, 1938, p. 55.

2. Harold F. Gortner, *Administration in the Public Sector*, New York: Wiley, 1977, p. 263.

3. Ralph M. Stogdill, *Individual Behavior and Group Achievement*, New York: Oxford University Press, 1959.

4. See, for example, J. Tiffin and E. J. McCormick, *Industrial Psychology*, Englewood Cliffs, N.J.: Prentice-Hall, 1965.

5. Robert B. Finkle, "Managerial Assessment Centers," in Marvin D. Dunnette (ed.), *Handbook of Industrial and Organizational Psychology*, Chicago: Rand McNally, 1976, pp. 861-888.

6. Edgar Schein, *Organizational Psychology*, 3d ed., Englewood Cliffs, N.J.: Prentice-Hall, 1980, pp. 22-24.

7. Douglas McGregor, *The Human Side of Enterprise*, New York: McGraw-Hill, 1960, pp. 61-76. Peter F. Drucker, *The Practice of Management*, New York, Harper, 1954.

8. William B. Eddy and Thomas P. Murphy, "Applying Behavioral Science to Urban Management," in C. Levine (ed.), *Managing Human Resources. Urban Affairs Annual Review*, vol. 13, Beverly Hills, Calif.: Sage, 1977, pp. 217-221.

9. Herbert H. Meyers, Emanuel Kay, and J. R. P. French, Jr, "Split Roles in Performance Appraisal," *Harvard Business Review*, January-February 1965, pp. 21-29.

10. Leland P. Bradford, J. R. Gibb, and K. D. Benne (eds.), *T-Group Theory and Laboratory Method*, New York: Wiley, 1964.

11. Frederick Herzberg, *Work and the Nature of Man*, Cleveland: World Publishing Co., 1966. See also "One More Time: How Do You Motivate Employees?" *Harvard Business Review*, January-February 1968, pp. 53-62.

12. Eric Trist, "Adapting to a Changing World," in George A. Sanderson

(ed.), *A New Role for Labour: Industrial Democracy Today*, Toronto: McGraw-Hill Ryerson, 1978.

13. Roy Payne and D. S. Pugh, "Organizational Structure and Climate," in M. Dunnette (ed.), *Handbook of Industrial and Organizational Psychology*, Chicago: Rand McNally, 1976, pp. 1125-1173.

14. U.S. Department of Health, Education, and Welfare, *Work in America*, Report of a Special Task Force, Washington, D.C., 1972. (Reprinted by the MIT Press.)

15. Eric Trist, op. cit.

16. Robert N. Ford, *Motivation through the Work Itself*, New York: American Management Association, 1969. Also see J. R. Hackman, "Is Job Enrichment Just a Fad?" *Harvard Business Review*, September-October 1975, pp. 129-138.

17. Joe M. Law, "Quality Circles Zero in on Productivity." *Management*, U.S. Office of Personnel Management, volume 1, Summer 1980, pp. 2-5.

18. Edwin A. Locke, "The Nature and Causes of Job Satisfaction," in M. Dunnette (ed.), *Handbook of Industrial and Organizational Psychology*, Chicago: Rand McNally, 1976, pp. 1297-1350.

19. Douglas McGregor, op. cit.

20. H. H. Meyer, E. Kay, and J. R. P. French, Jr., "Split Roles in Performance Appraisal," op. cit.

21. W. Clay Hammer, "How to Ruin Motivation with Pay," in *Compensation Review*, AMACOM, a Division of the American Management Association, 1975.

22. Edward E. Lawler III, "New Approaches to Pay Administration," *Personnel*, vol. 53, September-October 1976, pp. 11-23.

23. Carl F. Frost, John H. Wakeley, and Robert A. Rich, *The Scanlon Plan for Organization Development: Identity, Participation and Equity*, East Lansing: Michigan State University Press, 1974.

24. Felix A. Nigro and L. G. Nigro, *The New Public Personnel Administration*, Itasca, Ill.: Peacock, 1976, pp. 132-133.

25. John B. Miner and J. F. Brewer, "The Management of Ineffective Performance," in M. Dunnette (ed.), *The Handbook of Industrial and Organization Psychology*, Chicago: Rand McNally, 1976, pp. 995-1029. Also see J. B. Miner, *Introduction to Industrial Clinical Psychology*, New York: McGraw-Hill, 1966.

26. Jeffrey L. Pressman and Aaron Wildavsky, *Implementation: How Great Expectations in Washington Are Dashed in Oakland*, Berkeley, Calif.: University of California Press, 1975.

27. Peter F. Drucker, *An Introductory View of Management*, New York: Harper & Row, 1977, Chapters 9-12.

28. Richard M. Steers, *Organizational Effectiveness: A Behavioral View*, Santa Monica, Calif.: Goodyear Publishing Co., 1977.

29. Edgar Schein, *Organizational Psychology*, 2d ed., Englewood Cliffs, N.J.: Prentice-Hall, 1970, p. 120.

6

Leadership and Management

Leadership, management, supervision, administration: to most of us these terms connote the rewarding and challenging side of organizational functioning. Once the agency is conceived, planned, structured, staffed and equipped, and begins operating, it becomes a dynamic system. At that point some mechanism for monitoring and guiding its process becomes necessary. In virtually all organizations of any size this mechanism is what we call *management.* Management, as the term is used, may refer to a person, a process, and/or a set of specific techniques. And *how* management is practiced may vary greatly from person to person and situation to situation. Our goals in this chapter are (1) to understand more clearly the phenomenon of management, (2) to compare some of the possible variations in style and skill, and (3) to relate managerial behavior to group and organizational effectiveness.

The overriding premise in the field of management is that what the leader does has an important impact on the system. Many studies have investigated the relationship between leadership and member behavior. One of the classics was first reported in 1940 by Lippitt, and later by White and Lippitt.[1] Adult leaders of boys' clubs were trained in three different styles—authoritarian, democratic, and laissez-faire (uninvolved). Leaders were shifted from one club to another after six weeks, with each adopting a different leadership style at the time of the shift. Thus, each of the clubs was exposed to each leadership style under a different leader.

Trained observers recorded the behavior of the boys as they worked on projects within the social climates that evolved under each style.

The findings clearly demonstrated that changes in leader behavior had a marked effect on climate. In the autocratically led groups (regardless of which leader was in charge) there was more dependence, less individuality, more discontent and hostility, but a somewhat greater quantity of work. In the democratic climates work motivation, originality, group-mindedness, and friendliness were greater. Members tended to keep on working when the leader left the room—more so than in autocratic groups. There was a clear difference between democratic and laissez-faire groups. In the laissez-faire groups (in which the leader's behavior provided minimal direction or guidance) there was lower quality and quantity of work done, more disorganization, and more playing around.

Although they were conducted in somewhat artificial settings with boys rather than adult employees, the Lippitt and White studies have had a significant effect on thinking about leadership. They were carefully designed and controlled to provide comparative results, and they clearly demonstrated some of the possible effects of the various styles.

In a study in industry, one of the few real experiments conducted in operating organizations, work groups were secretly divided into those who would receive favorable treatment and those who would receive unfavorable treatment.[2] The favored groups were treated positively and helpfully and praised for their performance. The unfavored groups were treated negatively, criticized, subjected to frequent reviews, and put into irritating situations. The quality of work of the unfavored groups (as measured by number of assembled products requiring repair) began to fall off within the first three weeks. At the end of three weeks changes were initiated in the work (new products, new procedures, and so on), and the differential treatment was halted. Under the new conditions, the performance of the previously unfavored groups fell far below that of the favored groups. The authors pointed out that the groups under stress because of the behavior of their supervisors were much less able to adapt flexibly to change.

Following a review and analysis of over one thousand studies on leadership, Bass concludes, in regard to group effectiveness[3]

> If group effectiveness depends on the occurrence of interaction, it also depends on the occurrence of attempted and successful leadership, since leadership is interaction. The more difficult are the problems facing the group and blocking goal attainment or the less able the members to cope with their problems and reach their goals, the more leadership is necessary and likely to be attempted and successful.

The relationship between leader behavior and organizational effectiveness is, however, not always simple and direct. Although one observer, Gortner,[4] asserts that "The ultimate success of any public agency rests upon the leadership of that organization...," others are less convinced.

Cartwright and Zander point out that decades of research indicate that leadership and group effectiveness are not so clearly and directly related as many people believe. They assert that, "The belief that a high level of group effectiveness can be achieved by the provision of 'good' leaders, though still prevalent among many people concerned with the management of groups, now appears naive in the light of research findings."[5] We all know of football teams and companies and public agencies that remain ineffective in spite of new leadership—just as we know some who improve when changes are made at the top. So, how may we understand the relationship between manager or leader performance and organizational effectiveness?

What role does leadership play in the effectiveness of public agencies and what measures are possible to select or develop those kinds of leadership not likely to succeed?

Part of the problem lies in a rather wide collection of terms and lack of clear agreement about which means what. Terms such as management, leadership, administration, authority, power, and control are often used interchangeably. Some of the differences, however, are crucial, because the way a manager's role is constructed and viewed by himself or herself and others in the organization may make the difference between success or failure. The following scheme, based in part on the work of French and Raven, will define the terms the way we intend to use them.[6] We begin at the broadest level with the overall *managerial role* and look at its various components.

The Managerial Role

1. Formal Power-Authority
   a. Reward power
   b. Coercive (punishment) power
   c. Legitimate or position power
2. Leadership
   a. Referent or charismatic power
   b. Interpersonal competence
3. Expertise
   a. Subject matter knowledge
   b. Administrative skills
   c. Executive skills
4. Creativity and innovativeness
5. Personal motivation, energy, health
6. External power base

In performing in the managerial role the individual has several possible sources of *influence* on the functioning of others. (I prefer the term *influence* rather than control because it more accurately reflects the managerial reality. Many factors, including the manager, influence what happens; vary rarely does anyone have absolute control.) One category of sources of influence are those furnished by the organization itself—the authority to exert power through rewards, punishments, and application of rules, regulations, and laws. This first category is referred to as *formal* authority and is based on occupying a position at a given level in the hierarchy.

The second category covers those functions that may be viewed as *leadership*. They include referent or *charismatic* power (the ability to inspire the confidence and discipleship of others) and interpersonal competence (the ability to understand and interact successfully with other people). Leadership as a source of influence is less tangible and more individualistic than formal authority.

The third category, *expertise*, refers to knowledge about the work to be done and/or the functioning of the organization. Substantive knowledge deals with the work of the unit—taxes, supplies, economic development, and so forth. Administrative skills refer to those behaviors necessary to keep the organizational mechanism functioning on a day-to-day basis—work flow, systems and procedures, regulations, forms, personnel actions. Executive skills, on the other hand, go beyond day-to-day administration to broader areas such as planning, policymaking, resource allocation, and evaluation.

The fourth area, labeled here creativity and innovation, is an aspect of some managers' behavior that has recently been discussed by Zaleznik as being in marked contrast to what we described before as administrative skills.[7] It involves behaviors that foster new approaches, departure from traditional avenues, and the taking of risks. This person's energies go not into maintenance of the bureaucracy, but into entrepreneurial activities involving new goals and new approaches. (Unfortunately, Zaleznik chose to call this area "leadership," thus confusing it with the human motivation aspect of the managerial role. Perhaps the term "entrepreneurism" would have been more useful.)

Personal health, energy, and motivation are self-evident but often underemphasized factors in management performance. As public executive Harlan Cleveland points out

Almost any physical or mental illness diminishes vitality and heightens self-concern. For an executive, serious illness results in a lowered interest in his work, a tendency to shut out new information (he feels he has too much already), further analysis (the problems on his plate are already more complicated that the human spirit can bear) and uncomfortable peers (who likely will ask him to think some more rather than decide on the basis of what he already thinks).[8]

Organizations whose managers operate under high levels of stress are likely to underestimate its impact on performance and effectiveness. Most significant management roles are demanding and trying assignments. Any successful incumbent must have a strong desire for the rewards it offers and the energy and stamina to pursue those rewards.

Finally, in many administrative-political systems, managers may derive a portion of their influence from factors outside the immediate organization—political connections, community prestige, or wealth, for example. Such sources of influence can be troublesome for the organization because they often require some reciprocity from the manager, such as patronage jobs, favors, or time devoted to outside activities.

Some managerial situations provide all of the above sources of influence, some provide very few. A manager whose position and personal qualities provide many sources of influence has a good chance of having an impact on the unit. Consider an energetic manager who was selected because of demonstrated leadership qualities and who has received training to further sharpen these qualities; who is knowledgeable about the business of the unit, but also has well-developed administrative and executive talents; and whose role provides a good deal of latitude in the exercise of formal power—providing rewards (monetary and psychological), a discipline process with teeth in it, and the authority to create, change, and enforce rules. If there is any potential at all among the members of the unit, this manager should be able to call it forth.

Consider, by contrast, the all-too-typical government manager, often an individual promoted to a managerial position because of seniority or substantive knowledge of the unit's work, little demonstrated leadership performance, and minimal useful training. It's a managerial role in which virtually all of the rewarding, punishing, and regulating functions are tightly defined by statute and controlled by staff units such as personnel and human relations. Opportunities for executive functions such as planning and decision making are nil. Many such managers try to gain leadership skills—one of the few power options open to them—but do so ineptly by trying to be nice guys who don't push too hard or ask too much. Their major available avenue is administrative skill, maintaining and massaging the application of regulations, and keeping any disturbances in the flow to a minimum. Such a manager is likely to do little to enhance the effectiveness of his or her unit.

Thus, there are managers who are not leaders, and leaders who are poor managers, but there are few highly effective managers who do not have strong leadership qualities as well as roles containing adequate authority. Clearly the limiting factors on the impact of leadership are the degrees and kinds of power available to influence performance. When organizations move technicians with few leadership qualities into low power positions as a means of rewarding reliability and good technical performance, they are asking for ineffectiveness. And when these individuals attempt to overcome the limits of the role with supervisory practices manuals and short-term training sessions on principles of leadership, they are further confounding the problems.

The Federal Executive Service and Federal Executive Institute represent tacit acknowledgement by officials in the White House and the Office of Personnel Management that far too many high-level federal administrators are not managers. The political and civil service systems, the high level of technical orientation in many federal agencies, and the need to provide economic rewards by promoting individuals through managerial ranks combine to create this situation. Millions of dollars and thousands of employees are overseen by individuals whose personal qualities and roles do not contain enough of the power elements of management. One remedy is to attempt to create a cadre of high-level manager-generalists who view themselves as professional managers and who undertake the training and career development necessary to maintain their skills. Accompanying changes in the way the agencies view the roles of their top executive managers will also need to occur if the plan is to succeed. This is partly a political problem, since strengthening the bond of professional managers could mean lowering the influence of elected and appointed officials.

SITUATIONAL FACTORS

There are other limitations on the success of a given manager in a particular unit. Some of these we have discussed earlier, such as poorly designed tasks and cooperative systems, unqualified employees, unrealistic reward systems, and negative social psychological climates. These factors, plus others we will discuss shortly, provide the substance for what is referred to as the *situational view of leadership*. This view holds that Socrates was probably wrong when he asserted that a man with the right skills could be an equally effective head of a chorus, a family, a city, or an army. At least in this day and age Socrates' view appears oversimplified. Too many factors specific to a particular situation help to determine the success of a manager's attempts to influence a system.

Thus, we are left with the generalization that there is no formula for managerial effectiveness that can be applied across the board. Effectiveness will be determined by the following questions:

1. Does the role provide the manager influence over those decisions, policies, resources, and sanctions important to the success of the unit?
2. Does the manager have the personal inspirational and interpersonal qualities to exert leadership over the members of the unit and others in the system?
3. Does the manager have the necessary expertise about the business at hand as well as the system's administrative processes?

POWER DISTRIBUTION

Only one of the significant questions about power in management is the one we have been discussing—how much power does the manager have from the various sources within his or her role? Another equally significant question is the degree to which the power holder shares or delegates to others. Much of the recent writing about management has concerned itself with exploring the possible advantages of power-sharing techniques such as participative management and democratic group decision making.

It is evident, of course, that traditional managerial approaches that utilize hierarchical command systems and scientific management techniques concentrate power in the hands of the manager. In our earlier discussion of motivation we indicated that these approaches functioned by giving the manager power over the rewards (wages, conditions of work, and so on) and punishments (disciplinary action, firing, and so on). It is also evident to astute observers that there is a good deal of difference among managers in the way they use their power. Some seem to rely largely on punitive or coercive techniques and to get work done by threat. Others use mainly the positive sides of their power; and still others seem to use their power very little—at least not in obvious ways. Which strategy works best?

Researchers at the University of Michigan Institute for Social Research analyzed a number of different studies that compared the behaviors of two groups of supervisors—those deemed successful and those deemed unsuccessful. (Effectiveness was measured by a variety of criteria from one study to another.) The findings

System 1	System 2	System 3	System 4
Exploitive authoritative	Benevolent authoritative	Consultative	Participation-group

Figure 6-1 Likert's Four Systems

proved provocative. In the words of project director Rensis Likert

Two generalizations emerge from the results . . .
  1. The supervisors and managers in American industry and government who are achieving the highest productivity, lowest costs, least turnover and absence, and the highest levels of employee motivation and satisfaction display, on the average, a different pattern of leadership from those managers who are achieving less impressive results. The principles and practices of these high-producing managers are deviating in important ways from those called for by present-day management theories.
  2. The high-producing managers, whose deviations from existing theory and practices are creating improved procedures, have not yet integrated their deviant principles into a theory of management. Individually, they are often clearly aware of how a particular practice of theirs differs from generally accepted methods, but the magnitude, importance, and systematic nature of the differences when the total pattern is examined do not appear to be recognized.[9]

Basically, Likert's conclusion was that the effective managers practice a more participative, team-oriented approach that utilizes joint goal setting, two-way communication, and decentralized decision making. His findings led him to define a continuum of power centralization which has come to be referred to as the "four systems." System I, the most centralized, is called *exploitive authoritative*. In this approach one or a small number of people control the organization through a hierarchical command system. System II, *benevolent authoritative,* and System III, *consultative,* utilize progressively less centralization. System IV, *participative-group,* is most decentralized and engages in the most power sharing. (Likert readily acknowledges that earlier theorists such as Mary Parker Follett came to similar conclusions by other routes.) Figure 6-1 shows the four systems continuum.

There is more to the issue of power sharing than simply which strategy one chooses to adopt. The manager's personal decision is likely to be affected by his or her internal attitudes and needs as much as by external situations.

Douglas McGregor made a major contribution to management

thinking by exploring the assumptions managers make about their subordinates and the effect these assumptions have on their managerial behavior.[10] McGregor believed that underlying much managerial behavior are a set of implicit beliefs, which he labeled *Theory X*. Theory X has been widely quoted and often misinterpreted as being a theory of management, which it is not. Its basic tenets are that the average employee:

—dislikes work and will avoid it if possible,
—lacks ambition and self-control and prefers to be led,
—has a low level of commitment to the organization and its goals,
—has little creativity,
—resists change.

Therefore management must take a highly directive and centralized approach in which employees are coerced against their will to perform at acceptable levels.

It was McGregor's belief that if Theory X is an accurate picture of employee motivation (and to many managers it seems painfully accurate), the cause lies not in human nature, but with the way most organizations are run. To the extent that organizations appeal largely to the basic physiological and safety needs and do not provide for meeting some of the higher level social, ego, and self-fulfillment needs, employees respond in a Theory X fashion. Thus Theory X assumptions act as self-fulfilling prophesies in which employees become what they are assumed to be. The assumptions, therefore, discourage power sharing and encourage centralization.

McGregor believed that an alternative set of assumptions was a possibility. *Theory Y* would suggest that employees:

—do not inherently dislike work but have been turned off by the organizational climate,
—have the potential for commitment, self-control, and creativity,
—can, in the right environment, be effectively supervised in a much less close and controlling fashion.

He proposed greater decentralization and delegation, management by objectives, and participative management techniques such as the Scanlon Plan as beginning steps toward systems in which the

Theory Y assumptions might become valid descriptions of the motivation.

Data on the effectiveness of participative management and power sharing are supportive on the overall, but mixed. Reactions vary. Some see it as a near panacea. See Warren Bennis's *Beyond Bureaucracy,* for example.[11] Others have established their reputations as critics of the approach. Joe Batten, author of *Tough Minded Management,* is one of those who have capitalized on the fact that participative approaches may seem indecisive, soft, and unmasculine.[12] McGregor, Likert, and McClelland,[13] are very clear that their data do not suggest power-sharing methods should be weak or permissive, or unconcerned with effectiveness, but this point has been missed or ignored by some critics. In his last book, published after his death, McGregor discussed his views of the most effective management strategy. In his words, "Such a strategy is *not* permissive management, or soft or indulgent management. It includes clear demands for high performance, clear limits consistently enforced."[14]

It has become fashionable in some management circles to assert that participative methods have proved ineffective and are out of style. Certainly there have been situations where programs to install participative methods floundered. There are, however, a good many case examples of successful applications.

In a review entitled "Participative Management: Time for a Second Look," Albrook surveyed applications of participative management techniques—mostly in industry.[15] He concluded that the basic concepts and views of leadership and human motivation underlying many of the participative techniques are sound, but they are sometimes misapplied, and also they don't fit all people and situations. Problems in application have included moving too fast, using arbitrary and authoritarian methods to install democratic-participative activities, and inadequate skill building to support the efforts. Furthermore, some organizations seem much better suited to participative methods, for example, those that emphasize innovation rather than routine or control operations. Similarly, some people, both employees and managers, are probably more likely than others to respond well to being offered a share of the power. The thought of operating independently, with less direct supervision and structure, is not appealing to some people. They may find themselves upset and immobilized, and retreat to the position of saying, "Just tell me what you want me to do, don't keep asking me what I think!"

Initially participative techniques were probably more popular in industry than in government. There are, however, several published examples of efforts to utilize power-sharing techniques in the public sector. Golembiewski reports on a project to mold the new Metropolitan Atlanta Rapid Transit Authority into an effective "collaborative-consensual system."[16] Because of the agency's mission, which was to plan, construct, and make operational a metropolitan area bus and rail system within a very short time span, it was recognized that a nontraditional approach was needed. According to Golembiewski, the system was constructed so as to (1) "avoid the closedness and ponderousness of large-scale bureaucratic programs which tend to be hierarchy-serving and emphasize stability, and (2) approach the openness and agile pro-activeness of an organic system which is oriented toward problem-solving and emphasizes timely changes of complex, temporary systems." Table 6-1 describes the theoretical model that underlay the change program and defined the characteristics of the contrasting organizational systems.

The specific goal of the project was to build a team-oriented management system that was characterized by participation and free-flowing communication. Training sessions in team building and organization development and various follow-up activities were used to introduce the concepts. Resulting attitudinal changes were measured using the Likert profile of the four systems discussed earlier, a group behavior inventory, and also interviews. Managers in the organization moved in the direction of more open, participative norms, and also came to place higher value on system IV approaches to management. The advantages of such a system in a fast-growing, innovative public organization seemed well demonstrated. However, the project had not progressed far enough when the study was made to demonstrate whether the more participative attitudes and values actually affected the speed and quality with which the transportation services were developed.

The most current thinking about power sharing is that it is not possible to prescribe a formula for participative management that

Table 6-1   Dominant Characteristics of Two Opposed Ideal Managerial Systems

Coercive-compromise system	*Collaborative-consensual system*
Superordinate power is used to control behavior reinforced by suitable rewards and punishments.	Control is achieved through agreement on goals, reinforced by continuous feedback about results.
Emphasis on leadership by authoritarian control of the compliant and weak, obeisance to more powerful, and compromise when contenders are equal in power.	Emphasis on leadership by direct confrontation of differences and working through of any conflicts.
Disguising or suppression of real feelings or reactions, especially when they refer to powerful figures.	Public sharing of real feelings, reactions.
Obedience to the attempts of superiors to influence.	Openness to the attempts to exert influence by those who have requisite competence or information.
Authority/obedience is relied on to cement organization relationships.	Mutual confidence and trust are used to cement organization relationships.
Structure is power-based and hierarchy oriented.	Structure is task-based and solution-oriented.
Individual responsibility.	Shared responsibility.
One-to-one relationships between superior and subordinates.	Multiple-group memberships with peers, superiors, and subordinates.
Structure is based on bureaucratic model and is intendedly stable over time.	Structure emerges out of problems faced as well as out of developing consensus among members and is intendedly temporary or at least changeable.

Source: Based on Herbert Shepard, "Changing Interpersonal and Intergroup Relationships in Organizations," in James G. March (ed.), *Handbook of Organizations,* (Chicago: Rand McNally, 1965, pp. 1128-1131). See also R. T. Golembiewski and Alan Kiepper, "MARTA: Towards an Effective Open Giant," *Public Administration Review,* January-February, 1976.

fits all organizations and people equally well. A plan must take into account the history, task characteristics, personnel, and a variety of other factors. We will discuss these *contingency* approaches following the next section.

One emerging approach to power sharing is referred to as *industrial democracy*. In addition to management policies about employee participation, there is a movement, currently stronger in Europe and Japan than the United States, to include workers' participation in the "ownership" and policy processes of the organization. Such mechanisms as employee membership of corporate boards of directors, management-worker councils, and union participation in organizational decisions are sometimes mandated by legislation. Through such mechanisms, employees or their representatives become involved in discussing policies and structures as well as day-to-day operational problems. It seems likely that these trends will continue and will affect public as well as private organizations. Indeed, most public managers are well aware of government employees' increasing influence on their agencies. These developments attest to a growing tendency to view employees as *citizens* of their organizations with a rightful say-so in governance.[17]

Before leaving the topic of power sharing, a final point should be made. Not all observers agree that the question, "How much of his or her power should the manager share in order to maximize effectiveness?" is a proper question. To leave that question to the manager to decide as a matter of strategy implies not only that the manager "owns" the power, but also that the unequal distribution of power (the hierarchy) is legitimate. Frederick Thayer, for example, represents a point of view that advocates *An End to Hierarchy! An End to Competition!*[18] Hierarchy according to Thayer legitimizes inequity and encourages alienation from the organization. It really is not helpful in the long run, in his view, to pursue a democratic model in which those who hold the power decide when and with whom they want to share it, and when they will take it back. Scott and Hart worry about the fact that we are increasingly dependent upon large organizations and may begin to believe we must do whatever is necessary to keep them operating.[19] This puts great power in the hands of managers—perhaps power they will use to increase their control even further.

The concept of nonhierarchical organizations where power is equally distributed and all members act responsibly in the guidance of the system is an attractive idea to many. Perhaps such organizational forms are in our future, but examples of nonhierarchical systems of any size are rare today.

MANAGERIAL STYLES

We will now look at another of the significant frameworks that are being used to analyze managerial performance. In discussing the effectiveness of supervisors, Gellerman makes a useful distinction between *substance* and *style*.[20] Substance refers to *what* the supervisor does—the many administrative and technical tasks that are required by the role. Style, on the other hand, is a matter of *how* the supervisor goes about carrying out the tasks. Since the substance is specific to each supervisory role and varies greatly from unit to unit and organization to organization, textbooks and general training programs are not of great assistance to supervisors in that area. Most of the contributions of the behavioral sciences involve the area of *style,* including the analysis of the relationship between style and employee behavior.

In the 1950s the Bureau of Business Research at Ohio State University conducted a series of studies on leadership behavior.[21] Two separate style factors that subsumed most of the behavior of the leaders studied were identified. These were labeled *initiating structure* and *consideration.* Initiating structure referred to task-oriented behaviors such as establishing rules, setting deadlines, developing procedures, and evaluating performance. The consideration behaviors were people-oriented and included supporting and encouraging employees, developing a friendly atmosphere, and talking with workers about their needs and concerns. Some leaders tended to emphasize the task while others stressed a people orientation, and there was debate about which was most productive. Further research demonstrated that it is not necessary to follow one approach or the other exclusively, but that a style which emphasizes both the task and the people is feasible.

Robert Blake and Jane Mouton adapted these concepts and other related findings into a training model called the *managerial*

154 Public Organization Behavior and Development

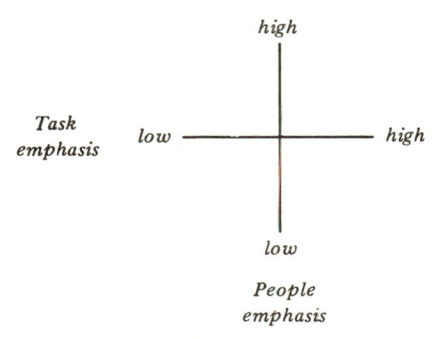

```
                        high
                         |
   Task        low _____|_____ high
 emphasis               |
                         |
                        low
                      People
                     emphasis
```

Figure 6-2 Dimensions of Leadership Style

grid.[22] By filling out a questionnaire about how to deal with various managerial problems, an individual receives a score that describes his or her style orientation. A high score on both the task and the people dimensions is viewed as indicative of greatest effectiveness. Other trainers and researchers including Hall and Hersey and Blanchard[23] have followed with similar conceptualizations—some allowing more room for weighing the impact of situational factors on style effectiveness. Figure 6-2 illustrates the general concept used by these authorities.

The two-style view of leadership behavior has been useful to managers because it has helped resolve the old dilemma, "Should I be hard-nosed, demanding, and task-oriented or is it better to rely on good human relations and try to gain productivity through positive motivation?" The findings are that, within certain limits, it is possible to develop a style which emphasizes task accomplishment and employee productivity while considering people's needs and promoting teamwork (the upper right hand quadrant of the figure). And further, it appears that this two-pronged style is often the most effective choice. Focusing only on the operational and mechanical aspects of the system (the lower right quadrant) is likely to bring on a fall-off in performance, for reasons this book has tried to make clear. On the other hand, running the work place like a country club, which avoids confrontation, conflict, and hard work (upper left quadrant) is likely to be equally ineffective. This finding is, of course, very much in concert with our sociotechnical systems view of organizations. Employees seem to be more productive and also to have more self-esteem when performance expectations are high but realistic and they are helped to attain the goals. Modifying the task focus with an understanding of people's motivation and the need to build in provisions for satisfactions (both intrinsic and extrinsic) is helpful, especially in today's society in which many people have come to expect consideration and attention to their needs in the work place.

The leadership styles concept can be translated from theory into practice through training programs that utilize style diagnoses questionnaires, group problem solving projects and feedback. At the Federal Executive Institute government managers participate in a week-long leadership styles workshop. Before being exposed to the underlying theory, participants fill out a questionnaire that examines their perceptions of their leadership and managerial behavior and they also work individually on case problems. They then learn about leadership style theory and work together in teams on simulated problems to perfect or modify their own styles. As is true in other external training settings, those participants who have colleagues who have also participated in leadership styles training are most likely to keep it in mind and find support and encouragement for applying it.

Based on running leadership style programs for a wide variety of managers, it is my belief that the most characteristic style for public administrators is not the high people, low task emphasis that many would predict. It is, rather, a middle ground or compromise stance that utilizes a modest amount of each emphasis (the middle point of figure 6-2). They emphasize task accomplishment enough to satisfy their supervisors but not enough to risk pushing subordinates too hard or stretching their own competencies. On the other hand, they try to use good human relations techniques with their subordinates, but do not commit themselves to basic team development, coaching, or rigorous performance evaluation. This fifty-fifty approach is encouraged by many norms in public organizations ("follow the regulations and don't make waves," "don't push too hard," "treat the people right and they'll cooperate"), but it is not the ideally effective style in most situations. It can make for mediocre, maintenance-oriented organizations in which external effectiveness is sacrificed for internal tranquility.

An interesting case is that of the manager who operates on the low end of both the task and the people scales. Such a nonmanager may be a professional or technical person who does not see himself or herself as a manager, a person unable or unwilling to be assertive and take risks, or a person with a boss so controlling and authoritarian that no significant authority and responsibility have been delegated.

SITUATIONAL CONTINGENCIES IN MANAGERIAL PERFORMANCE

By this point the reader has probably already anticipated one of the major problems in applying leadership theory. The determination of the optimum amount of power sharing and the best mix of leadership styles cannot be made once and for all for all situations. The underpinning research by Likert and others describes general trends and statistical significance, but there are exceptions. Many authoritarian managers are not highly successful, but some are. A highly task-oriented style with little understanding of the human element is not a recommended approach, but it does work well in some circumstances. The question that has occupied leadership researchers is how, beyond the useless generalization "it depends on the situation," to a set of more helpful principles about which approach works best in what set of circumstances.

Situational Leadership

Of the various approaches to understanding the situational variables in effective leader behavior, the research of Fred Fiedler is among the most long-term and substantial.[24] Over the course of many years he has analyzed the relationship among style characteristics, situational factors, member morale, and productivity. The three situational variables, or contingencies, that emerge from Fiedler's work are degree of *task structuredness* of the work group (workers know exactly what to do and how to do it), leader *position power* (authority to control, reward, and punish), and the quality of *leader-member relations*.

Under some combinations of these factors, task-motivated

leaders have been shown in Fiedler's studies to be most effective. In highly favorable situations (those in which leader-member relations are good, the task is structured, and the leader has a good deal of power) the task-motivated leader does best. Interestingly, in highly unfavorable situations (poor leader-member relations, unstructured task, low position-power) the task-motivated leader also seems to do best. A little thought will suggest possible reasons why these outcomes occur. In the highly favorable situation all the cards are stacked in favor of high performance. Since leader-member relations are already good and the task is structured, the leader is most efficient when emphasizing results rather than relationships. In the highly unfavorable situations, for example, an unpopular committee chairperson of a volunteer community betterment committee with poorly defined goals, the leader is better off emphasizing the task—hoping that focusing on the pursuit of the goals will motivate members and overcome the deficits in rapport and power.

In settings where the situational factors are mixed and neither highly favorable nor highly unfavorable, the relationship-motivated leader seems to do best. That is, when relations with subordinates are good, but task structure and position power are low, or when relations with subordinates are poor, but when task structure and position power are high, a focus on the human elements in the situation seems to be most productive. Since this mixed set of circumstances seems typical of a majority of leadership situations, the relationship-oriented position is probably most often the best strategy.

It is Fiedler's contention that since effectiveness of leadership depends upon the interaction between the leader's personality and situational factors, the appropriate match between the two is necessary. Since what we have termed "leadership style" is viewed by Fiedler as dependent upon basic personality structure and thus very difficult to change, the better option is to shift leaders around in order to match their established personalities with the contingencies of the situation. Leadership training, in Fiedler's framework, should focus on helping would-be leaders to diagnose their own styles and understand the kinds of situations in which they will likely be successful.

Style as a Decision-Making Strategy

Another contingency model that seeks to determine the best match between leader behavior and situational factors, but which assumes much more flexibility on the leader's part to shift styles, has been developed by Victor Vroom and Philip Yetton.[25] They follow a line of reasoning proposed by March and Simon[26] and others which views leadership as largely a sequential decision-making process. That is, the leader faces a certain problem or situation that requires a decision about what to do. Once that decision or choice is made, it affects the course of the process and soon leads to another choice point—and another and another. If the leader's style or strategy leads to the correct set of decisions, the problem will be solved in an optimum manner.

Vroom and Yetton propose five possible "decision processes" (which we have referred to as styles) which range from a highly autocratic approach, in which the manager gathers his or her own data and makes a unilateral decision, to a democratic approach, in which the manager chairs the meeting while the group reaches a decision by consensus. They are similar to Likert's four systems of management. The manager has seven situational variables to decide about. The first three have to do with the *quality* of the decisions and the last four with employee *acceptance* of the decisions. In analyzing the quality aspects of the problem the manager asks (1) Is quality (or correctness) crucial to the solution (for example, as opposed to equity or speed)? (2) Is adequate information available? (3) Is the problem structured? The next four choice points are: (4) Is employee acceptance necessary for implementation? (5) Would a unilateral decision be accepted by employees? (6) Do employees share the organizational goals involved in the decision? and (7) Is conflict among the employees likely in relation to the solution? As the manager wends his or her way through the process of weighing the situational choices, the model prescribes which of the styles (decision processes) will be most effective and timely in a given situation. In some situations, for example those which are highly structured and in which employee acceptance is unnecessary, a nonparticipating, unilateral decision is more likely to work. In other situations where no one individual has all the necessary information and high levels of employee commitment and follow-through are crucial, a participative decision is recommended.

Vroom and Yetton's approach to management training involves teaching managers how to use the contingency model, scoring them on their solutions to various organizational problems, and working in small groups with other managers to compare solutions and exchange feedback about working styles. Vroom and Yetton's data indicate, in disagreement with Fiedler, that managers utilize more than one style and that they are able to change styles when a change is clearly indicated. They admit, however, that changing one's approach in actual organizational situations is often difficult.

A Tridimensional Leadership Model

Hersey and Blanchard have contributed two additional concepts to the situational or contingency views of leadership.[27] One is an *effectiveness dimension* for the task orientation–people orientation scheme and the other is the concept of *maturity* as a crucial situational variable.

It has been observed by several leadership theorists that not only are there situational factors that affect the success of a given style, but that style combinations (such as high-task, low-people orientations) fit certain situations better. For example, a high-task, low-people style is probably best for a fire chief at the scene of a fire, but the opposite style might be most effective for the same individual at a later point when the unit's performance at the fire is being critiqued in a training session. Hersey and Blanchard have proposed that a third dimension, *effectiveness*, should be added to the task-people division and have described conditions under which certain styles may be effective and ineffective. Effectiveness in this context is a question of the appropriateness of the style to a given situation. Their work also points out the need for flexibility in adapting one's style to the demands of a particular situation.

Hersey and Blanchard have identified what they believe to be a crucial situational factor. They assert that *maturity* of the employees, individually and as a group, is important in determining which style to use. Maturity is specifically defined as "the capacity to set high but attainable goals, willingness and ability to take responsibility, and level of experience and/or education"—all these in relation to the task to be performed. The relationship between maturity level and most appropriate style is somewhat complex. It is, in fact, curvilinear. Employee groups who are low in maturity can best be dealt with by a high-task, low-relationship emphasis (for example, a group of underachieving school children). For groups with moderate levels of maturity a balance between task and relationship emphasis is most appropriate. Highly mature groups can best be led by a style low on relationship emphasis and low on task. Thus a group of mature and responsible professionals functions best when it is delegated a good deal of authority and responsibility for setting goals, designing tasks, and dealing with its own members. Too much management on either the task or relationship dimensions is likely to interfere and be resented.

Other Contingencies

Before leaving contingency theory it is well to be aware that there are other factors which need to be considered that are inherent in the situation. Among these are the fact that contingencies vary from one part of the organization to another, from one problem to another, and from one day to another. Scientists in the research and evaluation section may require a different style than do the janitorial force. Clerks whose work is highly repetitive may not understand why their supervisor functions differently from a manager of a group of program development specialists, but the differences may be necessary. As organizations grow more complex and the work of subunits more varied, it may be useful to promote the understanding that there is no single managerial style that will be used unswervingly across the board.

Managers in public agencies need to pay particular attention to the contingencies inherent in their administrative-political systems. We have discussed earlier some of the constraints on the public manager's behavior. Laws, regulations, and controls enacted by legislative bodies and commissions severely restrict one's options for taking action. Norms, habits, and political currents exert further pressures. And the expectations and demands of external

Leadership and Management 161

groups such as the media, the public, and special interest groups contribute to the field of contingencies that public managers must take into account. One of the problems for committed and competent public managers is to sort out the real from the imagined contingencies. Is there really no power to set high standards, evaluate performance rigorously, and weed out incompetents, or are the pressures against such actions largely informal norms born to keep things safe? Are the tasks so structured that there can be no participative decision making, or is low participation due more to managerial laziness or lack of skill? Is the apparent psychological immaturity of some subordinates a permanent condition, or is it possible to initiate developmental programs that will build maturity and thus the level of responsibility? Is there danger that the unilateral application of power may elicit short term efficiency while sacrificing the longer term development of capable personnel and a climate of commitment?

Another issue for the public manager is his or her own flexibility in changing leadership style to fit the contingencies of a given situation. We may laugh at the TV dilemma of the military officer who tries to run his family as he does his regiment, or the plodding government bureaucrat who is elected president of the PTA and bogs it down in red tape. Less funny are the federal officials from Washington, used to a well-controlled and formal internal administrative climate, who try to meet with hostile community groups and find that the ground rules have changed. Or the politician used to a free-flowing and unstructured work style who accepts an appointment as head of an organization that employs many people in routine paper-processing operations. Each needs to detach ego from style and realize that an approach that works well in one setting may need to be drastically altered for another setting.

Before leaving the present topic, it is important to touch on the question of values and ethics. Contingency theories are based on scientific and amoral concerns with predicting outcomes based on given inputs. There are, however, several issues that ought to be considered by the manager before deciding how authoritarian or democratic to be. Are there limits to which the ends justify the means? Is "whatever works" the appropriate guideline? Is long-

Table 6-2 Summary of Contingency (Situational) Factors in Choosing a Leadership Style

Fiedler

Degree of task structuredness
Leader position power
Quality of leader-member relations

Vroom and Yetton

Importance of quality of decision
Adequacy of information
Structure of the problem
Necessity of employee acceptance
Probability of employee acceptance of unilateral decision
Degree to which employees share organizational goals
Likelihood of conflict among employees

Hersey and Blanchard

Employee maturity (individual and group)
    Goal setting
    Responsibility
    Experience/education

Others

Work norms of employee group
External expectations and pressures
Managerial flexibility and willingness to risk

---

term commitment in danger of being sacrificed for short-term efficiency? Can trust be built if the manager listens to employees only when their follow-through is needed? Is consistency important in managerial style, and when does consistency become rigidity?

Millar believes it is still questionable that a managerial approach based purely on contingency theory would be workable. He proposes the establishment of levels of employee participation and shared authority which are at least minimally acceptable in terms of the value systems of those involved. Decisions based on contingency models would always allow, then, for a basic level of employee involvement.[28]

MANAGERIAL SKILLS

In spite of the generally accepted principle that there are no absolute, inborn *traits* of leadership, and in spite of all the work on situational factors, the belief still persists among some, including this writer, that there are some qualities that are *more likely* to characterize successful than unsuccessful leaders-managers. At the risk of appearing to offer formulas, in this section we will explore some of the qualities that seem to be most likely attributes of successful leadership in many, if not all, situations.

Diagnostic Ability

Whether or not he or she consciously operates with a contingency model, the effective leader needs to size up the situation continually, figure out the state of the various subsystems, and understand what the problems are and why they are occurring. Otherwise success is a matter of luck. Schein has called attention to the need for diagnostic skill, especially in view of the complexity and variability of human behavior in organizations.[29] One value of diagnostic skill is that it enables managers to perceive and understand important differences in motives of subordinates, rather than make the erroneous assumption that everyones' motives are similar.

Understanding of Self and Role

Effective managerial functioning in varied and changing settings requires that the manager have a clear understanding of his or her strengths, weaknesses, styles, emotional responses, biases, and impact on others. If a manager wishes to work out a practical theory of management to help in decisions and priorities, that theory should contain a subtheory of one's self. Otherwise the view is incomplete. Similarly, a manager needs a good understanding of his or her *role*. That is, what is expected, what objectives should be sought, how is the role perceived by others? For example, a manager who perceives his or her role as only maintaining the status quo when superiors expect significant change and improvement is likely to expend energy on the wrong issues.

Social Engineering

The emphases on decision making and problem solving sometimes make it seem as though management is primarily a sequence of unrelated acts. Nothing could be farther from the truth. Today's well-conceived plan to seek a group decision on a certain problem will be a total failure if yesterday's behavior, and last month's and last year's, did not contribute to the development of a team that is willing and capable of making good decisions. In many subtle ways, the manager's day-to-day behavior contributes to the social-emotional climate. Is it supportive and team-oriented, as Likert recommends, or punitive and divisive, for example? Morale, trust, cohesiveness, communication, and other important social variables are significantly influenced by the manager—whether by intention or not. It is better to know what kind of climate is most desirable and develop a strategy for pursuing it actively. In times of organizational crisis too many managers fruitlessly try to build trust and rapport overnight, hoping employees will forget the past years of unconcern.

Differentiated Role

Likert's research indicates that successful managers play a role that is clearly different from their subordinates' roles. Pitching in and being "just one of the men" is usually not the best approach. The effective manager is more likely to spend his or her time training, coaching, setting standards, planning and scheduling, and developing evaluation processes.[30]

The Linking Pin Function

Effective managers in complex public organizations must concern themselves with more than the internal workings of their own unit. Because organizations are open systems with interrelated parts in interaction with outside forces, managers serve as "linking pins" to connect their units with others. Among the necessary functions are staying aware of significant environmental factors and ability to interpret them to the members of the unit, functioning as a communication link with other systems, advocating the unit and its needs and contributions to superiors, and representing the unit at meetings to build cooperation.

Substantive Knowledge

Most of our discussion of managerial performance has focused on style rather than substance (utilizing Gellerman's distinction, which we referred to earlier). There is a point or two to be made about the manager's need for knowledge about the technical or mechanical aspects of the unit. On the day-to-day job, style and substance are not as clearly separated as they seem when we write about them. Most often style will show up in relation to the way the manager works on substantive problems. How does one conduct a meeting that is called to iron out an operating problem? How does one work with a subordinate who makes operational errors? How clearly and specifically are objectives established and pursued? The preponderance of opinion seems to be that the manager does not have to be the most knowledgeable person in the unit about the substance of the work, but he or she should probably have at least average knowledge, and, more importantly, the manager should see that the necessary information is readily available when needed.

MOTIVES OF SUCCESSFUL MANAGERS

In addition to skills and styles, are there other attributes of successful managers? For example, are their motives and goals different from those who are less successful?

Psychologist David McClelland has provided perspective on the question of power needs. Utilizing special tests, McClelland and his colleagues have measured managers' needs for power and also their needs for affiliation (friendly relations with others) and for achievement. Intensity of power needs varies from one individual to another. That is, some individuals' desire for power is great, and they will expend much more effort to gain and wield influence than will others. As one would predict, managers have higher power needs than do nonmanagers. Managers with extremely high power needs are not as likely to be willing to share that power through delegation and participation.

In a recent series of studies McClelland and Burnham discovered some interesting characteristics of successful managers' need systems.[31] The good managers in McClelland's sample had higher power needs and lower needs for affiliation than did less successful managers. They were more concerned about influencing other people than they were about being liked by subordinates. However, they also had other distinguishing characteristics. Their power needs were not oriented toward personal aggrandizement and dictatorial methods, and they were more mature and less egotistic. They focused their influence on the good of the organization and used it to help their subordinates feel strong and effective. Thus the psychology of power sharing takes on a new twist through McClelland's research. Those who function most effectively do not reject power; in fact, they seek it. But they utilize it in nonautocratic ways to improve the work climate and build teamwork.

Hall reports another interesting series of findings about managers' motives.[32] Data gathered on 11,000 managers assessed their success in career achievement and also motivational and managerial style factors. Higher achieving managers favored blending people and task emphases, openness and sensitivity to employees, and participatory practices. There were some interesting differences between needs of low achievers and high achievers. The low achievers were more self-centered and were oriented primarily toward meeting safety and comfort needs. They engaged in behaviors aimed at defense and self-preservation. The high achieving managers, on the other hand, were characterized as other-directed and as seekers of the higher level needs such as actualization, belonging, and ego status. It was important to them to find meaning in their work and to impart meaning to others. Two of the most significant parts of Hall's findings dealt with the manager's own theory of motivation and with the impact of the manager's style on subordinates. Hall says

The manager's view of motivation—of what is important to his subordinates and of what is possible in the way of satisfactions within the organization—is a critical component of the motivational process. Depending on his view, the manager can create conditions for need satisfaction co-incidental to desired performance or he may frustrate and block needs along with the expression of the very skills of which his subordinates are most proud.

In one sense, both the Hall and the McClelland studies reinforce Fiedler's view that leadership training is of limited value because managerial behavior rests on personality characteristics that are hard to change. Motivational qualities such as need for achievement, and power and willingness to take risks are unlikely to be affected by a thirty-minute training film. On the other hand, both authors have developed educational programs designed to bring about the behaviors and the underlying attitudinal changes needed to move toward effectiveness in their models. It is to this important aspect of the managerial field that we turn in the next section.

MANAGEMENT DEVELOPMENT

We have devoted this chapter, as well as segments of earlier parts of this book, to the exploration of skills, styles, attitudes, and strategies that may increase the manager's ability to perform effectively. For those people whose behavior already fits the models, the chapter should be a pleasant affirmation. But what about those of us not lucky enough to be born into families that ingrained in us the proper behavioral skills? Or not fortunate enough to have happened into educational experiences or relationships with mentors which led to effective styles becoming a part of our natural behavior? Is it possible to learn what we need to know, and, if so, how?

Management development, that subfield of training devoted to helping people learn how to manage, is at best a mixed bag. Traditionally, since organizations and their managers were viewed as logical and rational, management development programs have focused on providing factual information, principles by which to manage (planning, organizing, controlling, and so on), and analytic techniques. This approach is no doubt the most widely used in both agencies and academic programs in public administration. The problem is, however, that there is a sizeable body of evaluation research on training which indicates that while the learning of facts and principles may be a necessary prerequisite for functioning effectively as a manager, it is usually not sufficient. The personal qualities and interpersonal skills (including the style factors we have discussed in this chapter) are of major importance. And these cannot be taught simply by providing cognitive information and rational techniques—if, indeed, they can be taught at all.

It has been proposed that *manager development* is perhaps a more appropriate term to define that aspect of training to which we are referring. The manager functions as a total person, not just as an information source or decision maker. It is the individual, using himself or herself in all capacities—perceiving, informing, responding emotionally, empathizing, persuading, risking, confronting, decision making, evaluating, comforting, meeting, and on and on. Mintzberg studies what managers actually do and has identified three categories of roles: *interpersonal* roles, *informational* roles, and *decisional* roles. He found that "in all cases the interpersonal, informational and decisional roles were inseparable."[33] If this is true, then programs seeking to develop managers must blend the skill and knowledge from these areas, and treat them in such a way that the learning is *applicable* to real managerial situations.

It is beyond the purpose of this book to design or prescribe manager development programs. It is fair to say, however, that a program which truly provides the talent to meet the managerial needs of public organizations must consist of considerably more than occasional seminars on speaking effectively and management by objectives. The ideal program begins with an analysis of the managerial performance needs of the organization and its subunits (what does successful managerial performance consist of in this setting?) and a diagnosis of the learning needs and interests of each manager or trainee. The next step is a formal or informal development plan for each person. Only then can training programs be designed to augment the other possible learning situations (tutorials, on-the-job training, job rotation, university courses, self-study) needed to meet each individual's learning requirements. Training needs to offer learning on both substance and style, to build application skills rather than just information storage, and provide ample opportunity for practice and feedback about performance in order to correct errors.

Ideally, also, effective training does not end when the learner returns to work. The greatest payoff (perhaps the only payoff) comes when the new learnings are encouraged and supported on the job by colleagues and when all are striving to implement the same or compatible practices. Organization development (OD), a body of concepts and techniques aimed at enhancing work unit performance, is one approach to this problem. It will be discussed in the next chapter.

ETHICAL ISSUES IN PUBLIC MANAGEMENT

As we have shown in many ways in this volume, the public manager does not function in a vacuum. The environment is full of pressures and demands which converge on the manager and seek to influence him or her. How does one decide what is the *right* or *ethical* or *professional* course of action in the face of several alternatives? As events in the decade of the 1970s powerfully demonstrated, it is possible for public managers to do severe damage to their agencies, their colleagues, and their own careers when they confuse or disregard the ethical implications of an action. And perhaps most unfortunately, they despoil the rest of us in the public sector by reconfirming the all-too-common stereotype that we are all "on the take" anyway. The public manager who accepts a kickback from a supplier, does a political favor for a legislator in return for tangible or intangible reward, uses position power to elicit sexual relationships with a subordinate, or diverts the productive capacity of the department from assigned tasks to building his or her own image violates ethical standards as defined by the consensus of society or the legal process. Even in times of changing values the general dimensions of dishonest or unethical behavior are widely understood and agreed upon.

Approaches to encouraging higher standards of ethics in public agencies include: *values clarification*, a training program designed to help participants clarify their own personal values; *codes of ethics* which articulate for employees the agency's ethical standards and expectations; strong legal or administrative *sanctions* against unethical behavior; and various tactics to *reduce the opportunities* for people to engage in unethical behavior (such as the Hatch Act, which outlaws federal civil service employees' participation in partisan political campaigns). We shall briefly discuss the first approach: values clarification.

In the Watergate affair and in other cases of unethical behavior, it was found that many violators had never formulated personal ethical values which they could use to guide themselves when they were caught in value dilemmas. Thus they drifted little by little into situations and actions which they later regretted. Helping people think through and make operational their own ethical stances before the point of crisis is often helpful. This may be done in a training setting, through reading and discussing cases or essays dealing with ethical dilemmas, or by participating in exercises designed to help spell out one's values. Whatever the vehicle, it is important for an aspiring public manager to ask such questions as: "What are my long-term career goals in public management? What ethics and values do I believe in as I strive to reach those goals? What ethical dilemmas am I likely to encounter on the way? How will I choose to respond? A little reflection reveals that these questions are not far removed from the more basic question, "Who am I as a person?"[34]

THE CHALLENGE OF PUBLIC MANAGEMENT

Over the past decade and a half I have worked in educational settings with hundreds of men and women who hold responsible positions in public agencies. Those who function largely as *administrators* (maintenance, regulation, paper flow) by virtue of either self-concept or prescribed role are frequently bored and sometimes boring. On the other hand, those who see themselves as *managers*, who take responsibility, make decisions, motivate subordinates, and innovate, are rarely bored. They are, unfortunately, sometimes stressed. And they are usually busy and find less time than they would prefer to spend on their own development. Adding to the stress and overwork is that fact that managers in public agencies are called on to respond to factors often outside their control, including pressures from external groups, the need for significant organizational changes, cumbersome civil service systems, unpredictable budgets, fuzzy criteria of performance, and pressure to demonstrate tangible achievement at each public election campaign.

Harlan Cleveland, long-time public executive and statesman, writes about his view of the "future executive."[35] The organizational environment, he predicts, will be of increasing complexity, with tensions among the many elements, highly participative decision making, and less hierarchically structured. Clear distinctions between public and private enterprise will continue to blur and problems of values and the public good will be troublesome. About the managers who will be responsible for running the organizations of the future, Cleveland says: "The future executive will be brainy, low-key, collegial, optimistic, and one thing more— he will enjoy complexity and constant change."

We can only add that the future executive will also need the ability to apply the ideas, skills, and styles we have reviewed. No small challenge.

NOTES TO CHAPTER 6

1. Ronald Lippitt, "An Experimental Study of the Effect of Democratic and Authoritarian Group Atmospheres," *University of Iowa Studies in Child Welfare*, vol. 16, 1940, pp. 43-195. Ralph White and Ronald Lippitt, "Leader Behavior and Member Reaction in Three 'Social Climates'," in Dorwin Cartwright and Alvin Zander (eds.), *Group Dynamics: Research and Theory*, 3d ed., New York: Harper & Row, 1968.

2. S. Schachter, L. Festinger, B. Willerman, and R. Hyman, "Emotional Disruption and Industrial Productivity," *Journal of Applied Psychology*, vol. 45, 1961, pp. 201-213.

3. Bernard Bass, *Leadership, Psychology, and Organizational Behavior*, New York: Harper, 1960, p. 450.

4. Harold F. Gortner, *Administration in the Public Sector*, New York: Wiley, 1977, p. 238.

5. Dorwin Cartwright and Alvin Zander, "Leadership and Performance of Group Functions," in D. Cartwright and A. Zander (eds.), *Group Dynamics: Research and Theory*, op. cit., p. 301.

6. J. R. P. French and B. H. Raven, "The Bases of Social Power," in D. Cartwright (ed.), *Studies in Social Power*, Ann Arbor, Mich.: Institute for Social Research, 1959.

7. Abraham Zaleznik, "Managers and Leaders: Are They Different?" *Harvard Business Review*, May-June 1977, pp. 67-68.

172   Public Organization Behavior and Development

8. Harlan Cleveland, *The Future Executive*, New York: Harper, 1972, p. 76.

9. Rensis Likert, *New Patterns of Management*, New York: McGraw-Hill, 1961, p. 97.

10. Douglas McGregor, *The Human Side of Enterprise*, New York: McGraw-Hill, 1960.

11. Warren G. Bennis, *Beyond Bureaucracy: Essays on the Development and Evolution of Human Organizations*, New York: McGraw-Hill, 1973.

12. Joe D. Batten, *Tough Minded Management*, New York: American Management Association, 1963.

13. David C. McClelland and D. H. Burnham, "Power Is the Great Motivator," *Harvard Business Review*, March-April 1976, pp. 100-110.

14. Douglas McGregor, *The Professional Manager*, New York: McGraw-Hill, 1967, p. 78.

15. Robert Albrook, "Participative Management: Time for a Second Look," *Fortune Magazine*, May 1967, pp. 166-170.

16. Robert T. Golembiewski, "MARTA: Toward an Effective, Open Giant," *Public Administration Review*, vol. 36, 1976, pp. 46-60.

17. Carole Pateman, *Participation and Democratic Theory*, London: Cambridge University Press, 1970.

18. Frederick Thayer, *An End to Hierarchy! An End to Competition!* Second edition. New York: Franklin Watts, 1981.

19. William G. Scott and David K. Hart, *Organizational America*, Boston: Houghton-Mifflin, 1979.

20. Saul W. Gellerman, *The Management of Human Resources*, Hinsdale, Ill.: The Dryden Press, 1976, Chapter 3.

21. For a report of the Ohio State Studies see C. Shartle, *Executive Performance and Leadership*, Englewood Cliffs, N.J.: Prentice-Hall, 1956.

22. Robert R. Blake and Jane S. Mouton, *The Managerial Grid*, Houston: Gulf Publishing Co., 1964.

23. Paul Hersey and Kenneth H. Blanchard, *Management of Organizational Behavior: Utilizing Human Resources*, 3d ed., Englewood Cliffs, N.J.: Prentice-Hall, 1977. Jay Hall, "To Achieve or Not: The Manager's Choice," *California Management Review*, vol. 28, 1976, pp. 5-18.

24. Fred E. Fiedler, *A Theory of Leadership Effectiveness*, New York: McGraw-Hill, 1967.

25. Victor H. Vroom and Philip Yetton, *Leadership and Decision-Making*, Pittsburgh, Pa.: University of Pittsburgh Press, 1973.

26. J. G. March and H. A. Simon, *Organizations*, New York: Wiley, 1958.

27. P. Hersey and K. H. Blanchard, op. cit.

28. J. A. Millar, "Contingency Theories, Values and Change," *Human Relations*, vol. 31, No. 10, 1978, pp. 885-904.

29. Edgar H. Schein, *Organizational Psychology*, 3d ed., Englewood Cliffs, N.J.: Prentice-Hall, 1980. Chapter 6.

30. R. Likert, op. cit., p. 101.

31. David C. McClelland and David H. Burnham, op. cit.
32. Jay Hall, op. cit.
33. Henry Mintzberg, "The Manager's Job: Folklore and Fact," *Harvard Business Review*, July-August 1975, pp. 49-61.
34. For a description of value clarification training see Maury Smith, *A Practical Guide to Value Clarification*, San Diego, Calif.: University Associates, 1977.
35. H. Cleveland, op. cit., p. 89.

7

Organization Development and Change

Bureaucracies resist change. We talked earlier about the fact that bureaucracies are put together in such fashion that they maximize reliability and efficiency. One of the criticisms of bureaucracies at all levels of government is that they have been unable, or perhaps unwilling, to regear their modes of operation in order to cope more effectively with new conditions and new problems. Thus the challenge to the public manager is to not only maintain the daily operation of his or her unit, but also to administer in such a way that the organization remains viable and adaptive as the environment around it changes. These demands clearly demonstrate the need for the manager to develop knowledge and skills for coping with organizational change.

In addition to simply adapting to external changes, there is also the need to learn how to bring about positive and constructive renewal of the organization. This is a change problem also, but one of a different order. New ideas, new personnel, new technologies, and new methods provide opportunities for the organization to renew and enrich itself continually. If these possibilities are ignored, the organization may stagnate and fall behind. The importance of renewal as a part of the role of the manager is clearly a departure from the traditional view which emphasizes the belief that the manager's major responsibilities involve overseeing the ongoing operation of a previously established mechanical system, and acting only when something deviates from the prescribed approach. The public manager bears responsibility for a broader vision of the unit's progress and a more perceptive analysis of effectiveness. Organizational health must be defined in such a way that it involves more than immediate efficiency measures. It also must deal with the organization's long-term viability.

John Gardner spoke convincingly of the dangers of allowing the organization to stagnate and of the need for a continuing program of updating. In his book, *Self Renewal*, Gardner said

The same flexibility and adaptiveness that we seek for the society as a whole are essential for the organizations within the society. A society made up of arteriosclerotic organizations cannot renew itself.[1]

An example of an organization development and renewal project in a government agency is described by Kunde.[2] Dayton, Ohio, a progressive and middle-sized city, had a reputation for an efficient and businesslike government that took care of the daily needs of the citizens in the period preceding the 1960s. The government was organized as a "high quality and complex public utility." As the racial tensions, urban decay, and other complex social-economic problems of the decade began to make themselves felt in Dayton, the population began to decline, the tax base eroded, and the city's self-confidence began to slip. City Hall was not organized to deal with complex social and economic problems, only to deliver physical services such as street maintenance, utilities, and fire protection. As the problems mounted, it became clear that something outside the realm of the current city government needed to be done. The approach of many cities during that troubled decade was simply to graft on new and temporary organizational components using federal funds to buy the staff to attack various problems—usually in an uncoordinated fashion. The decision was made in Dayton, however, that a new form of organization and a new way of thinking about community problem solving was needed. The decision meant that the organization needed to be altered in its basic structure and problem-solving mechanisms.

The renewal effort began with a series of workshops for key supervisory and management personnel. Questionnaire data about city problems and needs were analyzed and participants were asked to focus on the kinds of measures that would be required in order to respond. The result of these efforts was a series of task forces composed of members whose jobs cut across a variety of the city's traditional departments. Each task force addressed a major problem area of the city. For example, there was a youth task force, chaired by the director of finance and composed of members from the various other city departments, such as engineering, legal department, fire department, and so on. An effort was made to provide a mixture of age, race, sex, and other employee characteristics on each task force. Contributors were selected in such a way that a variety of skills and knowledge about the city and its problems were present in each group. Task forces developed goals and work plans and met regularly to analyze the problem areas.

Kunde indicates that the team management program significantly altered the structure and operations of the city government. The collaboration of the city's traditional "line" departments on various community problems was assured by the cross-departmental membership on the task forces. Individual members of the city government had an opportunity to broaden their own understanding of the problems of Dayton and the ways in which their operating units could contribute to solutions. Forums were provided in which various points of view and interests could be articulated and negotiated. Although the task forces were originally designed to be only temporary modifications of the organization's basic structure, Kunde's assessment is that the task force and team management approach (which by now has modified into a still different organizational form) left a significant impact on the organization—a legacy that involves new ways of communicating among the various city departments and a considerably greater degree of involvement of employees at all levels in goal setting and problem solving.

THE CONCEPT OF PLANNED CHANGE

The Dayton example, plus many others, demonstrate that it is possible for government organizations to change and adapt effectively to meet new needs. Are such change processes to be understood as simply lucky accidents or the result of a particularly foresighted administrator, or are there techniques which allow a manager to increase the probability of effective adaptation to change?

It has been suggested that three kinds of change occur in organizations and society: *evolution, revolution,* and *planned change*. Evolution is a slow and often accidental adaptive process in which small successes and failures gradually lead the organization in the direction of a more effective approach. The problems with evolution are that it may not be fast enough to keep the organization viable and the end result is left to chance. Revolution, on the other hand, involves much more sudden and major changes in the organization—particularly in the leadership and control functions. Revolution is often the result of frustration or alienation of some segments within the organization or external to it. But simply changing the leadership of an organization often does not significantly change the organization's viability or its capability of dealing more effectively with problems. Social scientists have for some years studied the problem of change and explored techniques to go beyond evolution and revolution to planned change.

One example of effective planned change that has been studied extensively in the United States and elsewhere is the agricultural extension movement, which began operating in rural areas of the United States as far back as the late 1800s. Extension agents had as their goal the utilization by farm families of advanced knowledge and technologies in farming practices and home economics. In a series of carefully worked out programs they sought to implement their planned changes not by badgering the farmers to fertilize their crops or plant new hybrid seeds or by seeking legislation to force change but by involving themselves in the daily lives of the people in rural communities and winning their confidence and willingness to experiment. The highly developed technical state of American agriculture and its advances over other agricultural countries can be attributed in significant degree to the work of the agricultural extension agents.

In a pioneering book, Ronald Lippitt and his colleagues studied the role and behavior of individuals whom they called "change agents"—individuals whose roles were to facilitate change in the behavior of other people or organizations.[3] Change agents are consultants whose work involved helping other individuals or

178 Public Organization Behavior and Development

organizations address their own needs, face their own change problems, and work out their own solutions.

Timothy Costello, deputy mayor for administration of New York City, set down his thoughts about change processes that occurred in the New York City government at the time of Mayor Lindsay.[4] He identified five categories of change, viewed in terms of the factors that led to the change decision. The categories are

1. Planned Change. Change that comes about as a result of carefully thought out plans and principles—a fairly rare type of change.
2. Confluence of Forces. Some changes occur without prior intent when pressures and forces focus on an issue or problem area and trigger a change. By way of illustration the author points to eight forces that occurred together in 1967 to bring the decentralization of the New York School System—fund strategies, the mayor's philosophy, a Ford Foundation demonstration project, pressures from the black community, and so on.
3. Event-Dominated Change. Change may be brought about by a chain reaction of events. Each occurrence triggers a subsequent reaction until finally the organization is led to the brink of major change without preparation. For example, a breakdown in services in some unit may lead to citizen complaints, which cause a newspaper investigation, which leads to exposure of poor performance, which leads to resignations, and so forth.
4. Accidental Innovation. Unexpected ideas, proposals, resources, and combinations of people may lead the organization in a new direction or toward the solution of a long-standing problem.
5. External Intervention. Forces external to the organization may, of course, bring about change by imposing it (a topic we'll discuss later in this chapter). Such bodies may include legislatures, courts, other government agencies, or public officials.

ALTERNATIVES FOR PLANNED CHANGE

Leavitt has suggested that if you want to change an organization, there are three avenues to making the change.[5] These are (1) to change the structure, (2) to change the technology, or (3) to change people's behavior. In addition, it is possible to change the nature of the tasks employees perform, but these changes are often the result of the first three kinds of change. Although planned change strategies are a relatively new area of interest for behavioral scientists, the various techniques for encouraging intentional change have been around for some time. The most common avenue for attempting to change government agencies, including the federal government, has been structural change. *Reorganization*, as it is usually called, involves regrouping and sometimes redefining the functions to be carried out by various government agencies in such a way that responsibilities, reporting lines, communication channels, and other structural characteristics are changed. The assumption is that such structural changes will eventually bring about changes in the performance of individuals and an improvement in the efficiency or effectiveness of work. Attempts to introduce change through the introduction of technology are also not new. The computer is probably the most current example of the introduction of a new technology into an organization's operation in an effort to improve its performance. There is no question about the fact that the computer and other automated data-processing tools have been of major importance in encouraging organizational change. As most managers have discovered, attempts to change organizations by changing the structure or the technology are often not simple programs. As we have said before, organizations are complex systems, and change brought about in one aspect of the organization is likely to result in unanticipated changes at other places in the system. Thus there is frequently a social-psychological dimension to organizational change of any sort. It is to these behavioral aspects of change that we now turn.

Behavior Change

Not surprisingly, the emphasis in the remainder of this chapter will be upon Leavitt's third category of planned choice—changing the behavior of the people in the organization. Seeking to bring about change by focusing on the human element is often not as direct and clear-cut as structural and technical changes. In many cases behavior changes cannot be imposed in the same fashion that one would mandate a reorganization. As we have demonstrated in past chapters, management of people is not as simple as telling them what to do. Programs for bringing about changes of behavior in groups of people involve such activities as training and retraining, social system diagnosis, group problem solving, and various interventions that fall within the rubric organization development.

Before moving on it should be pointed out that none of the avenues to change is independent from the others. Structural changes are intended to affect behavior ultimately. Behavioral change efforts such as organization development may bring about rethinking of roles, practices, and relationships and perhaps lead to structural changes. Thus the distinction among the three avenues of change may be largely a matter of the decision about where to begin the change process. It also may involve assumptions about the basis of the problems that require change.

STRATEGIES FOR PLANNED CHANGE

Current theories and methods aimed at bringing about planned change in organizations trace their roots back to several earlier developments in the social sciences. Some of the major elements of these theories include group dynamics and sensitivity training, management consulting, counseling techniques, and the social-psychological theories of attitude change.

Management consultants have, of course, operated for many years in assisting organizations to improve their functioning. Consultants may have professional expertise in any one of a number of fields including engineering, accounting, management methods, or personnel. The major activity or intervention has tended to be the offering of expert advice. That is, the consultant brings into the organization background knowledge and/or skill that is presumably not possessed by anyone within the organization and makes such information available for the organization in its problem-solving activities. Such information can be highly useful to an organization if key members of the organization have made a thorough commitment to considering and using the information provided by the consultant and if the recommendations do not threaten the existing vested interests or ways of doing things too severely. Frequently the difficulty with management consulting is that findings are written up in report form and handed to some key member of the organization where they may sit unimplemented and gathering dust because they have not dealt with resistance.

Earlier attempts by social scientists to contribute to organizational change and renewal tended to emphasize the use of science but to remain somewhat uninvolved in the daily operations of the organization. Most such efforts fell into the following categories:

1. Training programs in which information and principles regarding human behavior are presented to managers in order to help them understand their peers and subordinates, and practice "better human relations," that is, to humanize the organization.
2. Attitude and morale surveys in which employee responses are gathered, summarized, and sometimes made available to management as well as incorporated into scholarly articles. (For example, Delbert C. Miller, "Using Behavioral Science to Solve Organization Problems," *Personnel Administration*, January-February 1968, pp. 21-29.)
3. Descriptive research studies that bear generalizations about various aspects of the organization. For example, employee response to change, problems of role conflict, leadership characteristics, and so on. (As in Robert Presthus, *Behavioral Approaches to Public Administration*, University of Alabama Press, 1965.)
4. The technology of personnel psychology has been applied in such areas as testing, performance appraisal, employee relations, and placement.
5. In addition, some consulting firms have utilized social science knowledge in their analyses and recommendations.[6]

Many of the current change strategies are oriented toward group activities. This is no accident. Some of the earliest work in this field was done by individuals whose interests were in group dynamics and adult education. In the 1940s these individuals, many of whom were related to a division of the American Education Association called the National Training Laboratories, experimented with group-oriented approaches to leadership training and attitude change and developed *sensitivity training*. Sensitivity training (or T-group training) is an educational method in which a small group of trainees engages in a relatively unstructured discussion process where the major topic under study is the social-psychological characteristics of the group itself. By participating in an intensive set of interactions related to the value system and problem-solving capabilities of a small discussion group, members are able to learn firsthand about the dynamics of groups as well as about their own styles and attitudes related to group participation. Those interested in organization change have learned to capitalize on the power of a cohesive and effectively functioning discussion group to solve problems and effect changes in attitude and perception.[7]

Social scientists have found out the hard way that simply providing research findings or sound scientific advice is often not effective in bringing about organizational change. For many of us, the world is too full of advice. We learn to defend ourselves against it and to rationalize our reasons for not accepting it. Furthermore, it often happens that advice from two or more experts about a particular problem varies considerably. Thus the manager who does want expert advice on solving organizational problems and bringing about changes still has the dilemma of deciding which of the recommendations to accept. Clearly, more effective strategies are needed.

A key point that has had some difficulty gaining acceptance is that there is an important skill dimension to bringing about organizational change. Individuals who are to operate in change agent or consulting roles can function more effectively if they have developed their own interpersonal and communication skills. A field that has made considerable progress in defining and developing such skill areas is the field of counseling. Counselors are taught skills having to do with listening, helping people analyze their own concerns and problems, providing support and encouragement in difficult situations, and creating interpersonal climates in which individuals find the safety necessary to explore possibilities of changing their perceptions or behavior. Such skill areas have become an integral part of the field of planned change. While it is true that interpersonal skills without a foundation of knowledge in organizational behavior and change processes leads to superficial consulting activities, it is equally true that social science knowledge without the skills of application often leads nowhere.

Yet another area important in the current practice of planned change has to do with the basic social-psychological data and theories relating to why and under what circumstances people change their attitudes, perceptions, and behavior. Social psychologist Kurt Lewin pioneered the research in this field. His students continued the work and were, as a matter of fact, some of the founders of the National Training Laboratories and the sensitivity group movement. Lewin believed that change as a human process needed study and better understanding, and he devised a number of ingenious experiments in which he could study the impact of change efforts. The important findings of Lewin and his followers included such principles as the importance of involving people in planning for changes that will affect them and the importance of understanding and dealing with barriers that arise in the process of attempting to bring about change.[8]

Still another field that supports change efforts and strategies is that of applied research. Scientists have always had an abiding faith that well-designed and executed research has the power to bring about change. This is presumably because scientific findings come as close to the truth as we know how to get, and also because of the supposed importance of our old friend rationality. Experiments conducted on feeding back the findings of organizational analyses to managers have indicated that if research findings are to be useful in organizational change, they must be accompanied by a set of techniques aimed at facilitating their acceptance in the organization. Under the terms *survey-feedback* and *action research* social scientists have perfected the process of helping organizations utilize scientific data to improve and correct their operations. In addition to standing on their own as planned change techniques these survey-feedback approaches have also assumed an important role in the broader framework of organizational change programs.[9]

ORGANIZATION DEVELOPMENT

Organization development, or OD as it is commonly called by practitioners, is a set of concepts and techniques comprising an overall approach to planned organization change. It utilizes a variety of scientific findings and methodologies, including those already discussed. Organization development goes beyond traditional training and consulting projects and attempts to help an organization establish and conduct a long-range process of self-evaluation and constructive change and renewal. One authority listed the following characteristics of the organization development process:

    a) A long-range effort to introduce planned change based on a diagnosis which is shared by the members of an organization.
    b) An OD program involves an entire organization, or a coherent "system" or part thereof.
    c) Its goal is to increase organizational effectiveness and enhance organizational choice and self-renewal.[10]

Although organization development projects vary considerably depending upon the style of the OD practitioner and upon the characteristics of the situation, the following generalized model of an OD program describes the progression of most such efforts fairly accurately:

1. A problem recognition stage in which the organization recognizes the fact that its productivity is being hampered by ineffective interpersonal relations or other kinds of socially related variables, and calls in outside consultants or addresses its own members to exploring these problems.
2. A data gathering stage in which interviews, observations, meeting analysis techniques, or other approaches are utilized to pinpoint difficulties involved in the organization's operation and provide suggestions for reasons for these difficulties.
3. A data analysis and feedback stage in which members of management are brought together and involved in reviewing the findings, diagnosing problem areas, and planning strategies for improvement and change.
4. The intervention programs that are designed to bring about desired changes may include meetings (on-site or at retreats) at which organizational members are helped to participate in developing new programs or new approaches to existing situations.
5. The responsibility for helping the organization come to grips with change problems and to work its way through the difficulties encountered is often assigned to someone in a change

agent role who is either a member of the organization or an outside consultant. This individual usually does not play the role of the expert advisor, but rather uses his or her clinical skills as well as his or her knowledge to help facilitate the problem-solving process of the group.
6. Members of the organization collaboratively develop procedures, policies, and norms that reinforce and implement the new ways of operating developed in the previous change efforts.
7. Training is an important component of OD. Ongoing programs integrated into the change process are made available to employees. Training methods tend to be participatory and experience-based. The laboratory approach of the National Training Laboratories (T-groups or sensitivity training) is frequently used to help employees develop interpersonal competence and teamwork skills such as group problem solving and decision making.[11]

Organization development differs from the more traditional management development and training approach in several ways. Perhaps most importantly OD attempts to change the total organization or one of its major subunits, whereas management development tends to focus more particularly upon individual managers and their knowledge and performance. Another distinction is that the organization development approach is group-oriented. Usually the focus of OD is a team, work unit, committee, or other such "organic" (naturally existing) group. Furthermore, while the substance of management development is usually a relatively abstract aspect of knowledge such as decision making, planning, or supervisory behavior, OD focuses on helping the organizational units learn by solving problems and dealing with issues that exist naturally within the organization. So, for example, an OD project might focus on the question "What barriers to communication does this unit face and what can be done to reduce or eliminate them?" rather than on a textbook theory of communication barriers.

Within the overall concept of organization development there are a number of specific techniques that a practitioner might pursue in order to deal with particular problems. For example, there is *action training and research*. As the name suggests, AT&R is an intervention method which combines training and applied research; but there are important added ingredients. Each stage of the process from initial contact through analysis and on to final evaluation is participative and devised to provide learning for both the client and consultant. AT&R is, according to Gardner, derived directly from Kurt Lewin's theories of change and is geared to create a set of conditions under which resistance to change is minimized. Briefly, the consultant and client enter into an agreement to examine jointly certain aspects of the functioning of the organization and to work together on solving problems that may be identified. As the project unfolds and problems are diagnosed, a collaborative process develops which provides the client maximum control over the research and training components and whatever new problem-solving programs or structures emerge from the project. AT&R has been tested in public organizations such as the California State Compensation Fund and several city governments and has proven to be an effective technique. The term *survey-feedback* is used to denote a technique that is similar to AT&R except that the data collection occurs through the use of a standardized questionnaire.[12]

Another common technology within the framework of organization development is team building. In team-building projects members of a group of people who work together (a management committee, a work unit, a group of directors that functions as a cabinet, and so on) meet together for an extended period of time, perhaps two or three days or more. Often the OD consultant has conducted premeeting interviews or collected data by questionnaires and is prepared to discuss with the team members the issues, problems, and needs that they themselves have identified as being important for the group to work on in order to improve its performance. The team then analyzes the ways in which members work together in their daily operations. The consultant plays the roles of helping individuals understand the interpersonal and group process problems that hinder their ability to work together and gain satisfaction and assists them to devise solutions to the problems that they identify.

Another set of OD technologies has to do with dealing with conflict. Techniques have been devised that help groups or individuals understand, confront, and work their way through conflicts and misunderstandings that hamper their cooperative efforts. Usually these techniques involve bringing the conflicting parties together under the guidance of the consultant who uses a variety of exercises and feedback tools to help them better understand the issues that divide them and then to begin to identify avenues for solving the problems and developing cooperation. Conflict resolution is one of the organizational problem areas about which structural views of management have relatively little to say. Thus, the OD technologies developed to help deal with conflict have been found to be useful in a variety of organizational situations.[13]

A "confrontation design" described by Beckhard brings conflicting units together for a short but intensive exploration of issues dividing two conflicting groups.[14] The underlying premise is that when groups are confronted with the impact of their behavior, they are motivated to look at alternative ways of functioning. Another design, a classic in labor-management conflict developed by Blake and Mouton begins by clarifying and testing the groups' cross perceptions.[15] And still another approach currently being tested is to have union and management representatives work together on projects which have value and meaning to both, such as devising ways to improve the quality of working life in the organization.

ORGANIZATIONAL CHANGE THROUGH JOB REDESIGN

Organization development strategies approach the problem of change by focusing directly on changing the people in the organization through providing them learning, new perceptions, attitude changes, and more effective ways of working together. These changes in the people may of course result indirectly in structural change. That is, they may result in reorganization of roles, positions, or tasks. Some approaches to change, however, attack the structural problem directly. These are the approaches that seek to bring about constructive change by redesigning and perhaps enriching the ways in which people's jobs are constructed. Thus, the design of work becomes the independent or causal variable and the individual's attitudes and reactions to his or her work become the dependent or resultant variables. In some ways, of course, approaches to job design trace their beginnings back to scientific management which taught managers how to use the sciences of the physics of motion and human physiology to design jobs in such a way that they were mechanically faster and more manageable. These approaches, it should be noted, focused primarily on adapting people to their work. They insituted programs for training individuals how to use proper motions and sequences of activities in order to perform tasks quickly and with least effort. Modern job designers pride themselves on taking a somewhat opposite approach. That is, they seek to redesign the nature of the job (number of elements, ease of performance, degree of interest and variety, and so on) so that the job better fits the psychological and physical characteristics of the human worker.

The sociotechnical systems model has provided the groundwork for many of the current approaches to job design. The work of psychologist Frederic Herzberg is also significant, as are recent efforts that involve the design of conditions to improve the quality of working life. Some of the early experiments in job redesign occurred in Europe in corporations such as Phillips, Volvo, and Saab-Scandia. In the United States major work has been done in the Bell Telephone System. Furthermore, it is reported that *job enlargement*, one of the predecessors to job redesign and enrichment, began in the early 1940s at IBM, where ways were sought to deal with employees' common complaint about doing the same task over and over again.

Work design efforts to improve productivity and job satisfaction as well as quality of work, absenteeism rates, and other less tangible factors tend to operate at three levels. At the first level are projects that study the specific jobs that employees do and attempt to restructure or redesign those jobs in such a way that employees find them a more positive experience. A second level of design has to do with the operation of working groups. In these projects team-oriented approaches to work are devised to help the working unit take greater responsibility for planning and organizing its own activities as well as performing the work and controlling for quality. The third level, which is often referred to as *organizational design*, focuses on some of the traditional concerns of the management scientists—communication channels, control systems, and organization of tasks. Current efforts at organizational design go beyond the more traditional approaches by utilizing modern concepts and technologies such as information systems, sociotechnical systems, and innovative structures like project teams and matrix organizations.

Work on the first level, that of redesigning specific jobs, is often referred to as *job enrichment*. Hackman,[16] who has studied job design extensively, identifies three psychological states that are critical in effecting the individual's motivation and satisfaction on the job. These are (1) *experienced meaningfulness* (importance, value, worthwhileness), (2) *experienced responsibility* (feeling personally responsible and accountable for performance), and (3) *knowledge of results* (regular feedback about how effectively one is performing the job). Job redesign-enrichment efforts seek to maximize these three factors and thus to improve satisfaction and level of job performance. Some job enrichment measures can be as simple as broadening workers' jobs by giving them a greater variety of tasks to perform and more responsibility for evaluating the speed and quality of their own performance. For example, clerical personnel who have been assigned to type only one kind of form again and again all day long might be given a variety of different kinds of typing assignments, and those assignments that are most difficult or boring might be rotated among all the typists so that each experiences not only variety but also a fair share of both the difficult and boring tasks. Another example is the transformation of an assembly line where each worker performs the same repetitive task many times an hour to a design in which the individual functions more as a semiskilled craftsman, taking responsibility for the assembly of a larger aspect of the product. Thus, rather than screwing nut A on bolt B all day long, an automobile assembly line worker might put together and install an entire electrical system in an automobile. Findings about the value of such job enrichment activities are fairly promising. There is evidence that redesign reduces boredom, cuts turnover and absenteeism, and raises job satisfaction. It frequently improves the quality of work done. In most cases, productivity stays at least equal and sometimes increases.

The second level of job redesign, that with a group orientation, takes into account social variables as well as the mechanical aspects of the job. One of the early and still classic examples of a group-oriented job redesign occurred in the British coal mining industry. Mechanization of the coal mines brought about a reorganization of the work methods. In the process, long-standing work teams were broken up and redistributed. These teams had not only worked together but had provided each other with safety and support under very adverse working conditions. After the break-up of the teams, researchers noticed significant increases in accidents, illness, and absenteeism. These human problems were clearly related to the loss of the close-knit working units. Experimenters sought to improve the work operations by redesigning the mechanized system to include new stable and autonomous face-to-face working teams. These new teams, once they became established, were helpful in rebuilding social support in the organization. These studies, conducted by Trist and others, provided some of the early foundation for sociotechnical systems theory.[17]

The third level of design intervention is the total structure of the organization. The goal becomes redesign of the system in ways that maximize the utilization of human resources, improve efficiency, raise productivity, or improve morale and worker motivation. System design techniques may range from traditional reorganizations involving redrawing the organization chart to more contemporary concepts like information processing and sophisticated control systems. In a survey of approaches to organization design, Pugh identified six primary dimensions of organization structure pertinent to consider from a design perspective. These are as follows:

Specialization—the degree to which an organization's activities are divided into specialized roles.
Standardization—the degree to which an organization lays down standard rules and procedures.
Standardization of employment practices—the degree to which an organization has standardized employment practices.
Formalization—the degree to which instructions, procedures, etc., are written down.
Centralization—the degree to which the authority to make certain decisions is located at the top of the management hierarchy.
Configuration—the "shape" of the organization's role structure, e.g., whether the management chain of command is long or short, whether superiors have

limited span of control—relatively few subordinates—or broad span of control —a relatively large number of subordinates, and whether there is a large or small percentage of specialized or support personnel. Configuration is a blanket term used to cover all three variables.[18]

There are many examples of organizational redesign in government, but most have to do with changing the structural configuration. A seemingly endless series of studies and proposals involving the reorganization of the federal government (and also governments at other levels) are based on the belief that changes in the communicating and reporting structures will bring about improvements in effectiveness. They wrestle with questions about whether or not there should be a separate United States Department of Education, whether the Park Service and the Forest Service should be combined, or whether restructuring and renaming the Civil Service Commission will actually result in changes in the behavior of members of these organizations and thus in improvement in overall performance. Whether changes in the structure actually bring about improvements depends to a significant degree on whether the original problems that cause losses in performance are due to structural inadequacies. It seems a fairly safe assumption that an organization with too many levels in the hierarchy is likely to find itself spending an inordinate amount of time trying to move business up and down through the organization. Similarly, an organization with too few levels may find its managers overburdened trying to supervise too many subordinates. It is also predictable that an organization with a highly varied mix of functions reporting to the same top level administrators is likely to have difficulty sorting out and addressing objectives and priorities. Structural reorganization in these cases is likely to be helpful.

There are other occasions, however, when structural reorganization may be nothing more than a smokescreen in which structural tinkerings are substituted for real solutions. Problems such as dealing with incompetent managers, redirecting the focus of the agency, loosening the influence of outside pressure groups, or correcting inadequacies due to lagging technology are not structural. There is likely to be a temptation to placate newspaper reporters, whose understandings of internal organizational workings may be

192 Public Organization Behavior and Development

superficial, by shuffling around on paper the various components of the organization while actually intervening very little in the daily operations.

In recent years the development of *matrix organizations* and *project teams* has provided useful avenues to organization design. These forms were originally devised to help in the management of large-scale projects in the defense and aerospace industries. An organizational problem of some significance in many situations is the tendency for individuals, especially professionals and specialized technicians, to become highly identified with their own functional units (research, design, planning, accounting) and have difficulty integrating their efforts with specialists in other areas when teamwork is needed to design or manage complex projects. Matrix structures attempt to solve this problem by making each individual a member of two primary work units. One unit is a project team that is formed for a specific duration of time to work on a particular project. The individual is also a member of his or her own functional professional group (design engineering, finance, and so on). In the matrix structure, the project team works on the project until it is either completed or moved to another part of the organization for another stage of its development. At that point the individual returns to the original functional unit to wait for reassignment to another project. The Dayton team management project described by Kunde earlier in this chapter is an example of a temporary system redesign. Like virtually every other intervention or redesign technique available, this one creates problems as well as solving them. Such systems are more complex, more difficult to manage, cause confusion about who one's primary boss may be at a given moment, and are difficult for people who do not function easily in ambiguous situations.[19]

MANAGEMENT BY OBJECTIVES

A currently popular change strategy is one to which we have referred in earlier portions of this book. *Management by objectives* (MBO) was originally introduced into industry as a technique for clarifying the work objectives of individuals and improving their work motivation by relating evaluation to achievement of participatively derived goals. MBO is currently being used in public organizations as a change technique aimed at helping agencies redirect their efforts.

Murphy describes the introduction of an MBO program into the government of a city of 100,000.[20] The project grew out of a management study which revealed that the patterns of communication among the twenty-three city departments and between the departments and the city manager and elected officials were muddy and confusing. In some cases departments that indicated they had close functional relationships with other departments found that those other departments did not express a reciprocal connection. Such a pattern made the processes of policy formation and implementation difficult and fraught with error. In an attempt to help the departments in the city gain additional guidance in terms of their objectives, roles, and relationships, a management by objectives program was initiated.

The program began with a two-day training session in which department managers participated in identifying departmental objectives and priorities and defining as clearly as possible both the perceived and the required relationships among the departments. This objective-setting process was then carried downward into the organization and two of the departments acted as pilot model units for further development of the MBO system. Evaluation indicated that after six months the participating departments felt they had improved their management substantially and were able to use the system in preparing budgets. These departments had better data with which to justify budget requests and were in a stronger position to demonstrate the impact of various funding decisions upon their operations. Another department of the city experimented with pushing the MBO process down to the very bottom of the organization. The solid waste unit developed pick-up targets for some of their crews, allowing them to leave for the rest of the day as soon as their assigned work is completed. Murphy says, "So far, the change has encouraged the employees to perform more work and finish it earlier—with fewer complaints of refuse strewn about the neighborhood than under the previous system." When MBO is based on behavioral science principles and is used as a participative technique for planned change, it can be quite helpful in integrating change goals throughout the organization. If it is thought of as a control technique and imposed unilaterally without appropriate participation, consideration of the needs and realities of each work unit, and attempt to identify and resolve resistances, it can at best have no impact (another one of "those programs that didn't work") and at worst can create a variety of negative consequences—confusion, lowered trust, extra paperwork.

IMPOSED CHANGE

One of the most common and difficult change problems has to do with changes that are imposed upon the organization from the outside without the participation of any members. In government such imposed changes may come from political bodies, courts, legislative actions, or decisions at higher levels in management. In these situations, the manager's problems are (1) to decide whether or not to accept the imposition of change (if such a decision is feasible), (2) to assist subordinates to understand and accept the imposed change, and (3) to install the new change with a minimum amount of disruption and resistance. In my experience, one of the great knowledge gaps in management is the belief that you can unilaterally impose change upon a segment of an organization and expect the change to be accepted and implemented. The fact is, of course, that employees in most organizations have a myriad of alternative ways of sabotaging, rejecting, and redirecting such imposed changes. They are most likely to take these actions when the changes threaten to endanger their security, their social relationships on the job, or their self-images as satisfactory employees. While it is *not* true that the average individual is resistant to change and afraid of new situations, changes that are not understood and/or threatening are not likely to be accepted readily.

Overcoming resistance to change is a topic that has been studied extensively in the past several decades. While it is risky to offer a formula for overcoming resistance, there are several measures a manager can take that will facilitate the acceptance of new technologies, methods, or structures. The most common prescription is to inform employees about upcoming changes as far in advance as possible. While communication is not a panacea for all resistance (uncertainty is only one of the causes), it is usually a good place to start developing the mutual trust necessary for successful implementation of change. Providing employees opportunity to participate in planning and implementing changes is one of the techniques for overcoming resistance which research evidence has supported. When one has an opportunity to participate in a process of implementing change, the feeling of loss of control is minimized and one can feel more optimistic. Another technique for dealing with resistance is to anticipate the ways in which the changes may negatively impact employees. For example, are the changes likely to disrupt long-standing work group or informal relationships? Will employees have a more difficult time achieving their previous level of performance and compensation? Will some individuals or groups be moved further from the center of decision making and communication? If these consequences can be anticipated early and their impacts softened or least discussed, there is a good chance of lowering some of the resistance. In the final analysis, however, no program for overcoming resistance can compensate for the lack of trust in a situation. If employees trust their management, if they feel that in the past their interests have been carefully considered, and if they have not experienced negative results from unannounced and unilaterally imposed changes, they are much more likely to face a new change with a minimum of resistance and a maximum of helpfulness.

THE MANAGER AS A CHANGE AGENT

Dalton reports an analysis of a group of studies describing successful change efforts.[22] The first stage in most change processes occurs when the development of dissatisfaction or tension within a system triggers the realization that things are not as they should be and that change is needed (labeled *unfreezing*). Once this realization takes place, success depends upon the "intervention of a prestigious influencing agent." At points at which there is dissatisfaction, uncertainty, and change, there is a strong tendency for people to identify with someone whom they perceive as having the capabilities of guiding them through the difficult period safely and successfully. Thus a respected and trusted individual can play a crucial role in the implementation of change. In some situations an outside consultant or counselor plays this role, for example, an organization development consultant, a therapist, or an agricultural extension agent, depending upon the level of the system in which the change is taking place. In many situations, however, the most available and most appropriate agent of change is the manager.

What attitudes, skills, and behaviors are most appropriate for the manager in facilitating the adoption of change successfully? While not exhaustive, the following list of attributes does demonstrate some of the important qualities of management behavior that are often helpful in bringing about change smoothly and with a minimum of resistance:

1. *Self-awareness.* Understands his impact on others in affecting their attitudes and behavior.
2. *Communication.* Helps others develop frank and open communication in which relevant information about needs, problems, and feelings is freely shared. Demonstrates his willingness to listen to and deal with such information.
3. *Diagnostic (rather than punitive) approach.* Encourages use of data (reports, measurements, etc.) for objective diagnosis and problem solving, rather than placing blame, punishing, scapegoating, etc.
4. *Conflict management.* Faces up to conflict and helps others deal appropriately with conflict situations involving important differences, issues, or feelings. Does not stir up conflict unnecessarily.
5. *Innovation.* Strives to build a system which encourages and rewards creativity, innovation, and risk taking. Minimizes punishment for failure of sincere efforts or ideas.
6. *Personal growth.* Places value on actively developing and on using new strengths and abilities—for himself and others.
7. *Support.* Works to build a positive climate of support, trust, and empathy.
8. *Group skills.* Functions effectively in group situations (meetings, etc.) to bring about positive participation and contribution of others.[22]

Much of the manager's behavior in dealing with change situations will rest with his or her basic managerial styles and attitudes about employees. For example, the Theory X manager whose style is highly task and control oriented is most likely to impose changes using a maximum of power and a minimum of participation. The Theory Y, people-oriented, participative manager is more likely to devise change strategies that seek to lower resistance and increase credibility and acceptance. There is no single style that is appropriate for all situations. A diagnosis of the trust and threat levels, the difficulty of implementing the changes, and the probabilities and costs of resistance need to be made before final decisions can be made about a strategy.

CONCLUSION

In this volume we have reviewed some of the ideas, concepts, and theories from both science and practical experience. They are designed to provide a degree of perspective on the increasingly complex role of the public manager. In the first chapter we discussed some of the problems, both internal and external, that are faced by contemporary public organizations. We noted that it is easy for the public organization to become inwardly focused, rule bound, internally blocked, and resistant to change. We saw in the first chapter and elsewhere that there is sometimes a tendency for members of public organizations to become confused about their mission and to be pressured into directions that do not meet the societal needs for which the agency was developed. Or they may be tempted to pursue personal goals to the exclusion of organizational goals.

We have further seen that by viewing organizations as sociotechnical systems, as collectivities of interdependent individuals and groups, we can understand some of the causes of the problems and develop strategies for dealing with them. These perspectives are fairly new to the study of management.

Earlier mechanistic and simplistic views of management ascribed the manager the roles of command and control. Management by exception was the byword. The manager saw that the system was set up (roles assigned, duties prescribed, and procedures set down) and then presided over the functioning of the well-oiled machine, stepping in when something went wrong, that is, when disciplinary action was needed, when something broke down, or when a new rule or procedure was required to cover a new problem. In modern organizations this reactive, control-oriented managerial role is usually not what is needed. The manager should be constantly diagnosing the state of the sociotechnical system, facilitating communication, improving the quality of the work climate, examining needs and possibilities for change, fostering processes of adaptation and renewal, and sponsoring training and development programs to provide the intellectual and psychological growth necessary to staff a renewing organization. Such a complex and demanding role cannot be played by a manager who is equipped only with simple formulas and prescriptions. The effective public manager must resolve to scan the environment continually for new opportunities and emerging problems, analyze the internal system on an ongoing basis, search for new techniques, points of view, and bits of knowledge wherever they may be found. He or she must also be open to the learning that comes from self-examination and feedback from others, and model the desirability of human growth by staying one step ahead of subordinates in the growth process.

NOTES TO CHAPTER 7

1. John W. Gardner, *Self Renewal: The Individual in the Innovative Society*, New York: Harper, 1965, Chapter 8.
2. James Kunde, "Task Force Management in Dayton, Ohio," in R. T. Golembiewski and W. B. Eddy (eds.), *Organization Development in Public Administration*, Part 2, New York: Marcel Dekker, 1978, pp. 219-226.
3. Ronald Lippitt, Jeanne Watson, and Bruce Westley, *The Dynamics of Planned Change*, New York: Harcourt, Brace and World, 1958.
4. Timothy Costello, "The Change Process in Municipal Government," in F. G. Brown and T. P. Murphy (eds.), *Emerging Patterns in Urban Administration*, Lexington, Mass.: D. C. Heath, 1970, Chapter 1.
5. Theodore Leavitt, *Managerial Psychology*, 4th ed., Chicago: University of Chicago Press, 1978. Chapter 25.
6. William B. Eddy, "Beyond Behavioralism? Organization Development in Public Management," *Public Personnel Review*, July 1970, pp. 169-174.
7. For background on group training and change see Edgar H. Schein and Warren G. Bennis, *Personal and Organizational Change through Group Methods*, New York: Wiley, 1965.

8. Lewin's contributions to training and change are documented by Alfred Marrow in *The Practical Theorist: The Life and Work of Kurt Lewin*, New York: Basic Books, 1969.

9. See Neely Gardner, "Action Training and Research: Something Old and Something New," *Public Administration Review*, vol. 34, March-April 1974, pp. 106-115.

10. John J. Sherwood, "An Introduction to Organization Development," Experimental Publication System, issue no. 11, American Psychological Association, 1971.

11. William B. Eddy, "Beyond Behavioralism?" op cit.

12. Neely Gardner, "Action Training and Research" op cit. For a description of a survey-feedback approach to organization development see David G. Bowers and J. L. Franklin, *Survey-Guided Development: Data Based Organizational Change*, La Jolla: University Associates, 1977.

13. One approach to conflict resolution is described in Rensis Likert and Jane Gibson Likert, *New Ways of Managing Conflict*, New York: McGraw-Hill, 1976.

14. Richard Beckhard, "The Confrontation Meeting." *Harvard Business Review*, March-April 1967, pp. 149-155.

15. Robert Blake, R. Sloma, and J. S. Mouton, "The Union-Management Intergroup Laboratory: Strategy for Resolving Intergroup Conflict." *Journal of Applied Behavioral Science*, vol. 1, 1965, pp. 25-57.

16. J. Richard Hackman, "Work Design," in J. R. Hackman and J. L. Suttle (eds.), *Improving Life at Work: Behavioral Science Approaches to Organization Change*, Santa Monica, Calif.: Goodyear Publishing Co., 1977.

17. Eric Trist and K. W. Banford, "Some Group and Psychological Consequences of the Long Wall Method of Goal Getting," *Human Relations*, vol. 4, 1951, pp. 3-38.

18. D. S. Pugh, "The Measurement of Organization Structures: Does Context Determine Form?" *Organizational Dynamics*, Spring 1973, pp. 19-34.

19. Chris Argyris, in "Today's Problems with Tomorrow's Organizations," describes some of the behavioral pitfalls of nontraditional structures. See *Journal of Management Studies*, vol. 4, 1967, pp. 31-55. (Reprinted in W. B. Eddy and W. W. Burke, *Behavioral Science and the Manager's Role*, Palo Alto: University Associates, 1980.)

20. William B. Eddy and Thomas P. Murphy, "Applying Behavioral Science to Urban Management," in Charles Levine (ed.), *Managing Human Resources. Urban Affairs Annual Review*, vol. 13. Beverly Hills, Calif.: Sage, 1977.

22. Gene W. Dalton, "Patterns of Organization Change," in G. W. Dalton et al. (eds.) *Organization Change and Development*, Homewood, Ill.: R. D. Irwin, 1970.

22. W. B. Eddy, "The Management of Change," in S. P. Powers, F. G. Brown, and D. S. Arnold (eds.), *Developing the Municipal Organization*, Washington, D.C.: International City Management Association, 1974, p. 157.

Index

Abilities, and organization behavior, 62. *See also* Skills
Accessibility, of public organizations, 7
Accomplishment, and effectiveness, 105
Action training and research (AT&R), 183, 186
Adams, John D., 55
Adaptive-coping cycle, 135
Administration. *See also* Management; Public administration
　vs. leadership, 28-29
　vs. management, 170
　and policymaking, 8
Administrative management approach, 24, 28
Aerospace industry, organizational structure in, 74
Age, and hiring practices, 13
Agencies. *See* Federal agencies; Organizations
Agricultural extension movement, 177
Albrook, Robert, 149
Alderfer, Clayton, 46, 47
Amtrak, 11
Androgyny, concept of, 56-57, 67
Argyris, Chris, 100

Army, U.S., 32
Assessment center, 109
Attitudes, employee, 51-52. *See also* Motivation; Values
Attitude surveys, 181
Authority
　in behavioral science, 35
　concentration of, 117
　formal, 142
　need for, 18
　and stress, 52
Automobile industry, job redesign in, 120-121, 189
Autonomy, individual, 117

Babbage, Charles, 24
Barnard, Chester, 34, 86, 105
Bass, Bernard, 141
Batten, Joe, 149
Beckhard, Richard, 187
Behavior
　changing, 179-180
　managing, 41-42
　multiple causalities of, 68
　nature of, 75
　predicting, 41
Behavioral science, applied, 31-37
Bem, Sandra, 56

Bennis, Warren, 149
Berne, Eric, 53-54
Beyond Bureaucracy (Bennis), 149
Beyond Freedom and Dignity (Skinner), 63
Biases, and organizational process, 96
Blake, Robert, 153, 187
Blanchard, Kenneth H., 154, 159, 162
"Blue collar blues," 119
Brown, J. A. C., 30
Bureaucracy. *See also* Organization
 hierarchical, 73-74
 and structured functionalism, 22-25
 use of term, 22
 Weber's view of, 22-23
Bureaucratic, label of, 81
Burnham, David H., 166

California State Compensation Fund, 186
Caplan, R. P., 54
Career development, 66-68
Cartwright, Dorwin, 141
Centralization, and job redesign, 190
Chain of command, 22, 24
Change
 behavior, 179-180
 in behavioral science, 34, 37
 categories of, 178
 event-dominated, 178
 inability to adapt to, 4
 kinds of, 177
 stress of, 140
 and work values, 98
Change, organizational
 imposed, 194-195
 through job redesign, 187-192
Change, planned
 alternatives for, 178-180
 concept of, 176-178
 OD approach to, 183-187
 strategies for, 180-183
Change agents, 177, 195

Checks and balances, concept of, 88
Citizens, employees as, 152
Citizenship
 and hiring practices, 13
 organizational, 12
City government
 AT&R in, 186
 cooperation in, 86-87
 MBO program in, 193
 renewal of, 175-176
Civil Service Commission, 27. *See also* Personnel Management, Office of
Civil Service Reform Act (1978), 125
Civil service reform movement, 27, 28
Civil service systems, 4, 8, 26-28
Cleveland, Harlan, 97, 143, 171
Climate, work, 94-95
 and human needs, 99-100
 and individual effectiveness, 116-119
 and leader behavior, 139-140
Coal mining industry, British, job redesign in, 190
Cohesiveness
 in organizational climate, 117
 in organizational process, 92
Collaboration, 87
 importance of, 5
 in OD program, 185
Collectives, organizations as, 197
Collusion, 88
"Command system," 28
Commitment, in organizational process, 91-92
Communication. *See also* Interaction processes
 breakdown in, 83
 importance of, 5
 interpersonal, 83-84
 networks for, 84-85
 openness of, 117
 and organizational change, 196
 in organizational process, 82-85
 problems in, 85

Complexity, and organizational process, 97
Computer, impact of, 179
Conditioning, 63
Configuration, and job redesign, 190
Conflict, 118
 in OD approach, 186-187
 in organizational process, 89-91
Conflict management
 and organizational change, 196
 techniques of, 91
Confrontation design, 187
Consideration, in organizational climate, 117
Construct, 43
Contingency theory, 156-160
Control
 atmosphere of, 9-10
 in behavioral science, 36
 in organizational process, 88-89
Control data, use of, 118
Cooperation. *See also* Interaction process
 in behavioral science, 36
 in organizational process, 86-88
Coordination
 vs. cooperation, 86
 need for, 29
Costello, Timothy W., 60, 61, 178
Creativity, in managerial role, 143
Cyert, R. M., 65

Dale, Ernest, 24
Dalton, Gene W., 195
Data gathering stage, 184
Dayton, Ohio, organizational renewal in, 175, 192
Decision-making strategy, style as, 158-159
Decision sciences, 25
Defense, perceptual, 60
Demands, organizational, 99-101
Democracy, industrial, 152
Design, organizational, 188
Development. *See also* Organizational development

management, 167-169
 orientation to, 117
 shift to emphasis on, 112-113
Deviancy, 40
Diagnostic ability, 163
Dissatisfaction, causes of, 46-47
Diversity, of public organizations, 7-8
Dixon, W., 30
Drucker, Peter, 111, 131, 132
Dynamics, intergroup, 99

Effectiveness, individual, 108-128. *See also* Employees
 ineffectiveness, 126-128
 and objective setting, 111-112
 and psychological contract, 110-111
 and reward system, 122-126
 task design and, 119-122
 and training and development, 112-115
 work environment and, 116-119
Effectiveness, managerial. *See also* Management
 determination of, 146
 development of, 128-129
Effectiveness, organizational, 129-135
 and adaptive-coping cycle, 135-136
 defined, 104-106
 and efficiency, 106-107
 factors contributing to, 134
 mixed criteria for, 107
Efficiency
 importance of, 28
 indicators of, 133
 nature of, 107
Efficiency experts, 119
Ellis, Albert, 54
Emotion
 and motivation, 42-50
 and perception, 58-59
Emotional styles, 55-57
Employee(s)
 attitudes and values of, 51-52

Index 203

as citizens, 152
on corporate boards, 12
ineffective, 126-128
motivation of, 148
and objective setting, 111-112
psychological contract with, 110-111
recruitment, selection and replacement of, 108-110
and reward system, 122-126
and task design, 119-122
and training and development, 112-115
and work environment, 116-119
Employee contract, in public organizations, 8. *See also* Psychological contract
Environment. *See also* Climate
in behavioral science, 37
and managerial role, 143
Esprit de corps, 21, 29
Ethical issues
and contingency theories, 161
in public management, 169
Executive(s). *See also* Managers
function of, 86
personalities of, 56
Expectancy theory, 48, 50
Expertise, in managerial role, 142

Federal agencies
managers in, 145
reorganization of, 74
reward systems of, 125-126
Federal Executive Institute, 67, 145, 155
Federal Executive Service, 129, 145
Federal government, organizational redesign in, 191
Feedback stage, in OD program, 184
Fiedler, Fred, 156, 157, 162, 167
Firing, alternatives to, 127-128
Flexibility
in leadership style, 161
in organizational style, 118

Follett, Mary Parker, 29, 147
Ford, Henry, 119
Ford, Robert, 121
"Formalistic impersonality," 94
Formality, vs. informality, 81
Formalization, and job redesign, 190
French, J. R. P., 54, 123, 141
Freud, Sigmund, 43
Fringe benefit programs, cafeteria, 123-124
Frustration-aggression hypothesis, 90
Functionalism, structured, 22-25, 72
Functions of the Executive (Barnard), 34
Fundamental Interpersonal Relations Orientation (FIRO), 89
Future Shock (Toffler), 13

Gardner, John, 175
Gardner, Neely, 186
Garfield, Pres. James A., 27
Gellerman, Saul W., 153, 165
General Services Administration, 101
George, C. S., 20
Gilbreth, Frank, 25
Gilbreth, Lillian, 25
Goal clarity, 118
Goal displacement, 132
Goal optimization, 133
Goals, in behavioral science, 35
Golembiewski, Robert T., 150
Gortner, Harold F., 106, 141
Government(s). *See also* City government; Federal government
administrative goals of, 3
"big," 97
criticism of, 4
organizational redesign in, 191
Griggs v. *Duke Power Company*, 13
Groups
interest, 8, 161
in organizations, 98-99
Group skills, and organizational change, 196
Gross, Bertram, 38
Gulick, Luther, 24

Hackman, J. Fichard, 48, 189
Hall, Jay, 154, 166, 167
Halo effect, 60
Hammer, W. Clay, 123
Hart, David K., 100, 152
Hatch Act, 97, 169
Hawthorne effect, 30
Hawthorne studies, 29, 31, 44, 98, 122
Health care institutions, 3
Hedonism, 43
Helpful mechanisms, in organizational process, 80-81
Hersy, Paul, 154, 159, 162
Herzberg, Frederick, 46, 47, 116, 121, 122, 188
Heterogeneity, of work climate, 118
Hiring decisions, 13
Human engineers, 119
Humanism, industrial, 13
Human relations movement, 28-31

Imperative, organizational, 100-101
Impersonality, formalistic, 23
Incentive systems
  group, 124
  pay in, 125
  piece-rate, 124
  vs. shared expectations, 30
  and work motivation, 47
Industrial democracy, 152
Industrial engineers, 119
Inference, 43
Inflexibility, 4
Influence, in managerial role, 88, 142
Informality, vs. formality, 81
Information, in behavioral science, 36
Innovation, 4. *See also* Change
  accidental, 178
  and organizational change, 196
  in managerial role, 143
Instincts, 43
Institute for Social Research, at Univ. of Michigan, 146
In-take process, employee, 109-110

Integration
  as dimension of achievement, 106
  of work climate, 118
Intelligence tests, 61
Interaction processes
  cohesiveness, 92
  commitment, 91-92
  communication, 82-85
  conflict, 89-91
  control, 88-89
  cooperation, 86-88
  intimacy, 93-94
  trust, 93
Interdependence, 77
Interest groups
  and contingency theory, 161
  and public organizations, 8
Interfaces, 78
Intervention(s), 76
  external, 178
  in OD program, 184
Intimacy, in organizational process, 93-94
Inventory, psychological, 89

Job enrichment-enlargement projects, 89, 189
Jobs. *See also* Employees; Work
  properties of, 117
  redesign of, 187-192

Kay, E., 123
Knowledge, substantive, 165
Knowles, Malcolm, 66, 67
Kunde, James, 175, 176, 192

Law enforcement agencies, cohesiveness in, 92
Lawler, E. E., III, 48, 57, 61, 123
Leadership. *See also* Management
  vs. administration, 28-29
  compromise in, 155
  and contingency theory, 162

emphasis on, 9
function of, 128
and group effectiveness, 141
importance of, 5, 14
in managerial role, 142
in organizational process, 81
situational view of, 145-146, 156-157
study of, 34
styles of, 139-140, 153-154
tridimensional, 159
two-style view of, 154
Learning. *See also* Training
adult, 66-68
concept of, 66
intentional and accidental, 65-66
and organization behavior, 62-65
Leavitt, Theodore, 178
Lewin, Kurt, 41, 186
Likert, Rensis, 81, 147, 156, 158
Line/staff relationships, 99
Linking pin function, 81, 164-165
Lippitt, Ronald, 139, 140, 177
Listening, active, 20
Local agencies, reorganization of, 74

McClelland, David C., 149, 165, 166, 167
McGregor, Douglas, 89, 111, 122, 147, 148, 149
Machiavelli, Niccolo, 21
Management. *See also* Public management
vs. administration, 170
administrative, 24, 28
by exception, 77
coercive-compromise system of, 151
collaborative-consensual system of, 151
control issues in, 89
defined, 139
importance of renewal in, 174
language of, 30
learning about, 14-15

origins of, 18
participative, 149, 150
power distribution in, 146-153
role of, 141-145
scientific, 25-26, 28, 119
situational contingencies in, 156-162
study of, 34
Management development, 167-169
Management by objectives (MBO), 89
and organizational change, 192-194
origins of, 111-112
principles of, 132
Manager(s). *See also* Public managers
as change agent, 195
motives of, 165-167
role of, 42
skills of, 163-165
styles of, 153-156
typical government, 144
March, Frederick, 65
March, J. G., 158
Marital status, and hiring practices, 13
Maslow, Abraham, 44-46, 47
Mass consent, principle of, 21
Matrix organizations, 74, 75, 192
Maturity
in leadership model, 159-160
of work climate, 118
Mayo, Elton, 29, 30, 31, 44
Meanings, importance of, 32
Media
and contingency theory, 161
and public organizations, 8
Membership, in behavioral science, 36
Merit pay, 126
Merit systems, 97. *See also* Incentive systems
in civil service, 26-28
importance of, 5
Meyer, H. H., 123
Millar, J. A., 162
Miller, Delbert C., 181

Miner, John B., 127
Mintzberg, Henry, 168
Mistrust, atmosphere of, 9-10
Money, as incentive, 122
Morale, 117
 as dimension of achievement, 106
 importance of, 5
Morale surveys, 181
Motivation
 Alderfer's model of, 46
 employee, 28, 148
 human emotion and, 42-50
 in Hawthorne studies, 29
 human emotion and, 42-50
 Maslow's model of, 44-46
 reward system for, 80
 study of, 32
 of successful managers, 165-167
 two-factor theory of, 46
Mouton, J. S., 187, 153
Murphy, Thomas P., 193

Nadler, David A., 48, 57, 61
National Association of Schools of Public Affairs and Administration, 129
National Training Laboratories, of American Education Association, 181
Naval Research, Office of, 31
Need hierarchy, Maslow's, 44-46
Needs, human, and organizational demands, 99-101
Networks, communication, 83, 84-85
Neurotic behavior, 53, 54
Nigro, Felix A., 125
Nigro, L. G., 125
Norfolk Naval Shipyard, quality circle at, 121
Norms, and deviancy, 40

Occupational Health and Safety Administration (OSHA), 82

OD *See*: Organizational development
Ohio State University, Bureau of Business Research at, 153
Operations research, 25
Organization(s). *See also* Public organizations
 change in, 177 (*see also* Change)
 as collectivities, 197
 effective, 129-136
 evolution of, 19
 failure of, 2-3
 groups in, 98-99
 informal, 30
 learning about, 14-15
 managing behavior in, 41-42
 matrix, 74, 75, 192
 model of, 78-82
 public vs. private, 10-11
 quasi-governmental, 11
 as sociotechnical systems, 38
 traditional models of, 77
Organizational development (OD), 15, 66, 87, 169
 and change, 183-187
 as training, 113
Organizational diagnosis, six-box model of, 79-81
Organization chart, 73
Organization design, explained, 33
Overspecialization, 119

Parsons, H. M., 31
Pasmore, W. A., 76
Patronage, 8
Pay. *See also* Incentive systems
 and effectiveness, 123, 125
 merit, 126
Payne, Roy, 116, 117
Pendleton Act, 27
Perception, 57-58. *See also* Psychology
 emotional, 58
 problems in, 60-61
 self-, 59-60
 situational influences on, 61

Performance, effectiveness as, 111. *See also* Effectiveness
Performance criteria, for public organizations, 7
Personality, executive, 56
Personnel Management, Office of, 108, 145
Piece rate system, 25
Planning, importance of, 5. *See also* Change
Plato, 119
Policy, 105
Policy implementation, as indicator of effectiveness, 130
Policymakers, and administrators, 8
Politics
 and organizational process, 96-97
 patronage, 26
"Polygluity," 97
POSDCORB (Planning, Organization, Staffing, Directing, Coordinating, Reporting, Budgeting), 24
Postal Service, 11
Power
 charismatic, 142
 distribution of, 146-153
 official vs. personal, 88
 sharing of, 151, 152
Prejudice, and organizational process, 96
Pressman, Jeffry L., 130
Presthus, Robert, 18, 181
Problem recognition stage, in OD program, 184
Problem solving, 4, 64
 formulas for, 65
 group, 114
Procedures
 in behavioral science, 33, 36
 need for, 18
 organizational, 78, 79, 95-98
Productivity
 developing strategy for, 48-49
 as dimension of achievement, 106
 and need satisfaction, 47-48

Professionalism, and organizational processes, 95-96
Profit, as indicator of effectiveness, 105
Progress, emphasis on, 9
Progressiveness, orientation to, 117
Projection, 60
Project teams
 vs. bureaucracy, 74
 and organizational design, 192
Psychological contract, 110-111, 133
Psychology
 adult learning, 66-68
 attitudes and values, 51-52
 emotional styles, 55-57
 emotion and motivation, 42-50
 learning, 62-66
 perception, 57-59
 personnel, 108
 self-perceptions, 59-60
 of stress, 52-55
Public administration. *See also* Administration
 embarrassing cases in, 131
 level of analysis in, 40
Public agencies, social forces affecting, 11-14. *See also* Federal agencies
Public managers, and contingency theory, 161. *See also* Managers
Public management, 1-3. *See also* Management
 challenge of, 170-171
 and collective bargaining situations, 12
 ethical issues in, 169-170
Public organization(s). *See also* Organizations
 accessibility of, 7
 defined, 2-3
 diversity of, 7-8
 human interaction in, 102 (*see also* Interaction processes)
 human problems of, 3-6
 specialization in, 4-5
 uniqueness of, 6-11

Public sector, effectiveness in, 105–130. *See also* Effectiveness
Public systems
  cooperation in, 86
  leadership in, 141
  vs. private, 101
Pugh, D. S., 116–117, 190
Punishments, 18
Purposes, in organizational process, 78–79

Quality circle, 121
Quality of working life (QWL), 120
Quality of Work Life Foundations, 12
Quasi-governmental organizations, 11

Race, and hiring practices, 13
Rational-emotive therapy, 54
Rationality, importance of, 28
Raven, B. H., 141
Recruitment, and individual effectiveness, 108–110
Redesign, organizational, 190–191
Regulations, in behavioral science, 36
Relationships, in organizational process, 81. *See also* Interaction processes
Reliability, of public agencies, 9
Religion, and hiring practices, 13
Renewal, importance of, 174
Reorganization, 179
Replacement, and individual effectiveness, 108–110
Resistance, dealing with, 195
Reward(s), 18
  formal, 122–126
  in organizational process, 80
  orientation to, 117
Risk, vs. trust, 93
Risk-taking, in organizational climate, 117
Roethlisberger, F. J., 29, 30

Role(s)
  differentiated, 164
  managerial, 141–145
  and perception, 61
  in public organizations, 4–5
  understanding of, 163–164
Role-playing, 114
Roosevelt, Pres. Franklin D., 28
Rules
  in behavioral science, 36
  need for, 18

Salary increases, lump-sum, 124
San Tzu, 20
Satisfaction, employee, 110
Scanlon, Joe, 124
Scanlon plan, 124, 148
Schein, Edgar, 110, 135, 136, 163
Schon, Donald A., 66
Schutz, William, 89
Scientific management, 25–26, 28, 119
Scott, William G., 100, 152
Security, employee overconcern with, 4
Selection, and individual effectiveness, 108–110
Self, understanding of, 163–164
Self-actualization, 45
Self-awareness, 60, 196
Self-image, 59
Self Renewal (Gardner), 175
Self-talk, 54
Seniority, importance of, 8
Sensitivity training, 114, 181–182
Service institutions, ineffectiveness of, 131–133
Sex, and hiring practices, 13
Sexual relations, in organizations, 94
Sherwood, J. J., 76
Simon, H. A., 65, 158
Skill evaluation plans, 124
Skill(s)
  and career progress, 2–3

leadership, 14
  managerial, 163-165
  and perception, 60
Skinner, B. F., 63
Social engineering, 164
Sociotechnical systems, 75-78
  collaboration in, 87
  communication in, 83
  cooperation in, 86
  groups in, 98
  intimacy in, 94
  open, 136
  organizations as, 38
Socrates, 20, 145
Span of control, 24
Specialization
  effectiveness and, 119
  and job redesign, 190
  in public organizations, 4-5
Spoils system, 8
  advantages of, 26, 27
  disadvantages of, 26-27
Stability, of public agencies, 9
Standardization, and job redesign, 190
State agencies, reorganization of, 74
Status
  differences in, 10
  and perception, 61
Steers, Richard M., 133-135, 136
Stereotypes, 60
  and organizational process, 96
  role, 57
Stogdill, Ralph M., 106
Stratification, in organizational climate, 117
Stress, 52-55
  and change, 140
  emotional, 59
  and managerial role, 143
Structure, in behavioral science, 33, 35
Structure, organizational, 72-75
  degree of, 117
  and environment, 82
  in organizational process, 80

  and planned change, 178-179
  in public vs. private systems, 101
Style, 153
  as decision-making strategy, 158-159
  emotional, 55-57
  leadership, 139-140, 153-154
Sunset legislation, 102
Superego, 43
Survey-feedback, 183, 186
Supervision, training for, 115
Support, 117
Survival, as criterion of effectiveness, 106, 136
System(s). *See also* Sociotechnical systems
  closed vs. open, 76
  concept of, 38
  of power distribution, 147
  public and private, 101-102

Task(s)
  in behavioral science, 35
  and effectiveness, 119-122
  specialization of, 118
Tavistock Institute, 76, 120
Tax revolt, 14
Taylor, Frederick W., 25-26, 30, 32, 119
Team building, in OD programs, 186
Team management program, 176
Teams, and job redesign, 190. *See also* Project teams
Technology
  in behavioral science, 37
  and planned change, 178-179
  and task design, 120
Telstar satellite communication system, 11
Tennessee Valley Authority, 11
Tenure, 27
T-group training, 114-115, 181-182
Thayer, Frederic, 100, 152
Theory X, 148-149, 197
Third sector, 3

Time and motion study, 25
Toffler, Alvin, 13
Tough, Alan, 64
Tough Minded Management (Batten), 149
Training. *See also* Learning
  in human interaction skills, 113, 114, 115
  management development, 167
  in OD program, 185
  for organizational change, 181
  role playing in, 114
  sensitivity, 114, 181-182
  technical skill, 113
Transactional analysis, 53-54
Trist, Eric, 116, 120, 190
Trust, in organizational process, 93
Two-factor theory, 46

Unemployment compensation systems, 13
Unfreezing, 195
Unions
  growth of, 24
  and management, 99
  public employee, 12
Unity of command, 24
Urwick, Lyndall, 24

Values
  changing work, 98
  and contingency theories, 161
  employee, 51-52
Values clarification, 169
Van Riper, Paul P., 28

Voluntary associations, 3
Volvo plant, task design in, 120-121
Vroom, Victor, 158, 159, 162

Wallen, Richard, 56
Watergate affair, 170
Weber, Max, 22-23, 27, 32, 33, 93, 119
Weisbord, M., 78, 79, 105, 128, 132, 135
Welfare, government employment as, 10
Western Electric Company, Hawthorne Plant of, 29. *See also* Hawthorne studies
White, Ralph, 139, 140
Wildavsky, Aron, 130
Wilson, Pres. Woodrow, 34
Work. *See also* Climate
  attitudes toward, 24
  and changing values, 98
Work culture, 95
Workers. *See also* Employees
  causes of dissatisfaction among, 46-47
  changes in lives of, 13
  and organizational imperative, 100
  in Taylorism, 26
Work life, quality of, 12

Yetton, Philip, 158, 159, 162

Zaleznik, Abraham, 143
Zalkind, Sheldon S., 60, 61
Zander, Alvin, 141